Shakyamuni Buddha

Artist: Chiang, Yi-tze

1

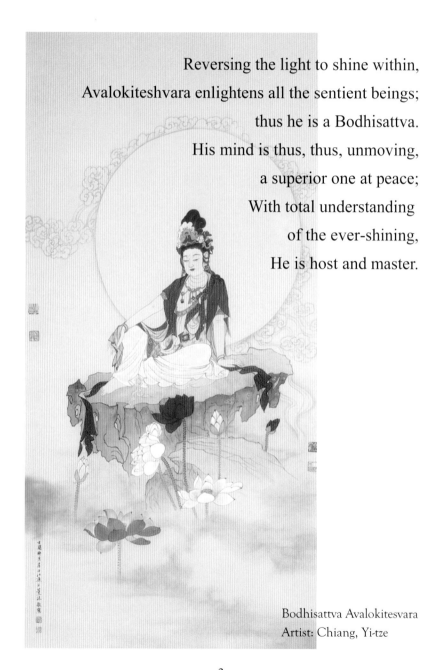

Reversing the light to shine within,
Avalokiteshvara enlightens all the sentient beings;
thus he is a Bodhisattva.
His mind is thus, thus, unmoving,
a superior one at peace;
With total understanding
of the ever-shining,
He is host and master.

Bodhisattva Avalokitesvara
Artist: Chiang, Yi-tze

2

Practice the Way, cultivate yourself,
And do not search outside.
The prajna of your own nature
is the deep and secret cause.
White billows soar to the heavens,
the black waves cease;
Nirvana, the other shore,
effortlessly is climbed.

Across the sea of suffering,
one leaves the revolving wheel.
The rains disperse, the heavens clears;
just then the moon is fully bright.
The qian source is the
way-substance,
among people the sage.
His undecaying golden body
is rare in the world.

Patriarch Bodhidharma
Artist: Chiang, Yi-tze

How does there come to be great wisdom?
Because the stupid make their mark.
Already in his mother's womb
  a fine eloquence had been born;
This real wisdom is complete within all people;
  Grasp it at Jewelled Wood Peak at Cao Creek.

Collection of the National Palace Museum,
Taipei, Taiwan. Republic of China

Mountains, rivers, and the great earth
  are only manifestations of consciousness.
"Dream, illusion, bubble, shadow" - so it is!
Be careful not to seek outside;
  maintain the Middle Way.
To cast down stained threads of cause
  is to come toward the Thus.

"Not defiled, not pure,"
   they are separate from corrupting filth;
"They neither increase nor diminish" -
   enlighten the dark and mysterious middle.
In the pure and deep ultimate silence,
   all creation is transcended:
A sudden awakening to the original perfect fusion
   of self and dharmas.

Collection of the National Palace Museum,
Taipei, Taiwan. Republic of China

For ten thousand miles the sky is clear,
   without a cloud or a shadow;
Still water fills a deep pool
   and reveals the light of the moon.
Like people who drink when thirsty
   and know the hot from the cold,
Talking about food, and helping it grow:
   the work is always wanting.

Each of the sufferings exerts preassure,

    and all attack together,

Accumulating is feelings which beckon,

    each unlike the other.

Only through extinction can the ultimate joy

    be attained.

Therefore, this is the Way that should be practiced to

    awaken to the emptiness of dharmas.

Artist: Chiang, Yi-tze

Through three turnings of the Four Truths
the Dharma wheel revolves,
Seven shares in enlightenment,
the Eightfold Upright Path,
intention, mindfulness and diligence.
One day connect right through
and ripen the fruit of sagehood;
Partial truth with residue is just a conjured city.

Arhats
Annonymous: Ming Dynasty
Collection of the National Palace Museum,
Taipei, Taiwan. Republic of China

There is no cultivation,
verification, or attainment.
What has characteristics and is
conditioned has a time of demise,
And Bodhisattvas, in becoming
enlightened to this truth.
Trust to prajna, and became even
with the other shore.

Bodhisattva
Avalokitesvara
Artist: Chiang, Yi-tze

The Storehouse-Teaching Bodhisattva:
six phenomenal paramitas.
The Perfect cultivates to the point
of wonderful enlightenment,
where noumenon is suddenly clarified.
Without any wisdom,
he destroys attachment
and empties every characteristic;
Without attainment,
he has no verification
and comprehends the
fusion of dharmas.

Bodhisattva Avalokitesvara with One Thousand Hands and Eyes.
Collection of the National Palace Museum,
Taipei, Taiwan. Republic of China

He makes a jeweled realm appear
on the tip of a single hair.
And he turns the Dharma wheel
while sitting on a speck of dust.
These words are spoken, yet few have faith;
I do not know how many know my sound.

Turning the Dharma wheel
Collection of the National Palace Museum,
Taipei, Taiwan. Republic of China

Having no impediments is the true letting go;
When fear is no more,
the activity-obstacles depart.
Distortion left far behind,
the characteristic of production perishes;
The coarse, fine, and dust-and-sand delusions of
your dream-thoughts become Thus.

Bodhisattva Avalokitesvara
Artist: Chiang, Yi-tze

Virtue is nowhere incomplete,
  and all the obstacles perish;
This final perfect stillness
  is called nirvana.
Those passed by,
  not yet come,
  and now existing,
All Buddhas of the
  three periods of time,
  rooted in a common source.

Sakyamuni Buddha
Collection of the National Palace Museum,
Taipei, Taiwan. Republic of China

The Venerable Master Hsuan Hua

The Heart of Prajna
Paramita Sutra

The Heart of Prajna Paramita Sutra

with "Verses Without A Stand" and Prose Commentary

with commentary by the
Venerable Master Hsuan Hua

English translation by the
Buddhist Text Translation Society

Buddhist Text Translation Society
Dharma Realm Buddhist University
Dharma Realm Buddhist Association
Burlingame, California U.S.A.

The Heart of Prajna Paramita Sutra
with *"Verses Without A Stand" and Prose Commentary*

Published and translated by:

Buddhist Text Translation Society
1777 Murchison Drive, Burlingame, CA 94010-4504

© 2003   **Buddhist Text Translation Society**
Dharma Realm Buddhist University
Dharma Realm Buddhist Association

First edition (USA) 1980
Second edition (USA) 2003

12 11 10 09 08 07 06 05 04 03   10 9 8 7 6 5 4 3 2 1

ISBN 0-88139-484-X

Printed in Taiwan.

Addresses of the Dharma Realm Buddhist Association branches are
listed at the back of this book.

Library of Congress Cataloging-in-Publication Data

Hsüan Hua, 1908-
  The heart of Prajna paramita sutra : with "Verses without a stand" and
prose commentary / by Venerable Tripitaka Master Hsuan Hua ; English
translation by the Buddhist Text Translation Society.-- 2nd ed.
      p. cm.
Translated from Chinese, originally in Sanskrit.
  ISBN 0-88139-484-X
  1. Tripiéaka. Sëtrapiéaka. PrajñÁpÁramitÁ. Hàdaya--Commentaries. I.
Tripiéaka. Sëtrapiéaka. PrajñÁpÁramitÁ. Hàdaya. English. II. Title.
  BQ1967 .H778 2003
  294.3'85--dc21

                                                    2002007274

Contents

Introduction One. vii

Introduction Two xviii

Introduction Three xxii

Eight Guidelines of BTTS xxv

Part I. The Heart of Prajna Paramita Sutra 1

Part II. A General Explanation of the Title. 3

    The Five Categories of Recondite Meaning 6

    The Five Periods of the Buddha's Teaching 14

    The Meaning of "Sutra" 16

    The Translator. 20

Part III. Explanation of the Meaning of the Text 23

    Prajna and Emptiness 29

    The Conditioned Body 35

    The Kinds of Suffering 40

    Shariputra 47

    Form Does Not Differ From Emptiness 51

    Feeling, Cognition, Formation & Consciousness 62

    The Emptiness of the Eighteen Fields. 78

    The Twelve Conditioned Causes. 84

    Emptying the Four Truths. 91

    No Understanding and No Attaining. 119

    The Meaning of Bodhisattva. 125

    Nirvana 138

    The Mantra 144

Part IV. Index 159

Introduction One

In uncountable ways this is an extraordinary book. It is one of those records of wisdom which can be consulted, just dipped into, or read through diligently many times over with inestimable benefit, because each repetition reveals to the reader a new depth or a new horizon. In a book ten times its length one could not fully praise its value as a key to the understanding of human life.

At the core of this book is the *Heart of Prajna Paramita Sutra* itself. In English a mere sixteen sentences, and a mere 262 characters in Chinese, the *Heart Sutra*, as it is called in brief, is nothing less than a summation of the wisdom of the Buddha. It distills perfectly the teaching of non-attachment, which is the doctrine of emptiness. As the Venerable Master Hsuan Hua says in his commentary, it is the heart in the heart within the heart. For more than two millennia it has been recited daily in Buddhist monasteries, convents, retreats, and households, in a practice which has continued to this day and now grows again on every continent of the earth. The human beings who have studied, memorized, recited, and treasured the *Heart Sutra* probably number in the billions.

The *Heart Sutra* is a summation, not an introduction. Yet precisely because it gives only the essentials, it is used in the Buddhist tradition as a text which aptly introduces the teachings to new students. Modern readers who are new to Buddhism can do no better than to begin their study with this volume. It is the presence of explanatory commentaries, however, such as the ones by the Venerable Master Hsuan Hua included here, that make the *Heart Sutra* so accessible to students, practicers of the Way, and to ordinary readers. Only the most advanced of masters can expect to grasp the full import of the sutra by itself without the aid of a teacher. Someone is needed who can explain the meanings that are packed so tightly together in the text. Indeed, not only the *Heart Sutra*, but all the Buddhist scriptures, from this the shortest one to the *Avatamsaka Sutra*, the most extensive one, are best studied with the aid of explanatory commentaries, which are given, either in spoken lectures or as essays or poems or interlineary glosses, by enlightened masters who have realized the principles of the sutras in their own lives.

Why is spiritual experience, rather than deep learning by itself, the traditional and the true prerequisite for a commentary on the sutras? Profound as the Buddha's teachings are, and difficult as their concise formulation in the *Heart Sutra* may seem at first, the teachings are not abstractions which can only be understood with the specialist's knowledge. The concern of the *Heart Sutra* and all the sutras the Buddha spoke is simply the life and death of living beings. What good is, what evil is, what the world is, why we are born in it and where we will go when we die, what we are to do with ourselves now while we are here, and how we can stop our suffering and find true happiness for ourselves and others: these are the questions that the Buddha answered. He spoke only about what really counts. In his own life, he gave up wealth, power, fame, and the pleasures that do not last, in order to attain what people really need: compassion and wisdom. He then spoke the sutras to teach others how to do what he had discovered how to do. If the sutras are books of knowledge, then, it is only in service of their higher purpose of being guides to life and death. And so to speak or write an explanatory commentary on one of the Buddha's sutras, one does not need to be a scholar, though scholarship may help—one can even, like the Great Master Hui Neng, the Sixth Patriarch in

China, be unable to read a word. What one must be is a master of life and death, one who has realized, in his or her own heart, what it really means to be a human being.

The two commentaries which are interwoven in the following pages, illuminating and making plain the subtle meanings of the *Heart Sutra*, are the work of the Venerable Master Hsuan Hua, Abbot of Gold Mountain Monastery in San Francisco and Tathagata Monastery at Talmage, California, Chairperson of the Sino-American Buddhist Association, and Chancellor of Dharma Realm Buddhist University. The Venerable Master combines in one person a scholar's mastery of the entire Buddhist Canon and a sage's mastery of the life-principles that the sutras contain. It is safe to say that this combination, not wholly uncommon during the centuries when Buddhism flourished in Asia, would nowadays be greatly difficult, if not impossible to find elsewhere than in the Venerable Master Hsuan Hua's teachings. In his two commentaries here—one in written verse, one in spoken prose—the Venerable Master holds up to the light of his knowledge and wisdom the sutra's jeweled sentences, so that each brilliant facet of the sutra shines on many different planes of the Buddha's teaching. The famous Buddhist lists—the Eight-fold Upright Path, which belongs to the Thirty-Seven Categories of Enlightenment; the Four Truths; the three sufferings and the eight sufferings; the three obstacles, the eight winds, the six basic and twenty subsidiary afflictions—these and others are explained clearly and in detail in this volume. So also are the Sanskrit words which have already been accepted into English as hallmarks of a supreme and ancient tradition—Buddha, Bodhisattva, Dharma, Sangha, Arhat, samadhi—and the doctrines which have already begun to change the mental landscape of the modern West: karma, precepts, respect for life, leaving home, enlightenment. Throughout all the clear and lively, sometimes humorous, sometimes arresting explanations, the Venerable Master never fails to lead the reader back to the sutra's central teaching of non-attachment, which is the basis of the compassion and wisdom of enlightenment.

The Venerable Master Hsuan Hua's birth itself was an extraordinary beginning. In a dream, his mother saw Amitabha Buddha emitting a brilliant light that pervaded the entire world, and she awoke to give birth to the Master while a rare fragrance lingered in the room. He was only eleven when he resolved to devote his life to cultivating the Buddha's Way. While out playing with friends, he saw the dead body of a baby girl, and not knowing what it was, he ran home to ask. A friend of the household informed him that death is inevitable for everyone, unless they are able to end the revolving wheel of birth and death by following in the footsteps of the Buddhas. He immediately resolved to leave the home-life to become a bhikshu, a Buddhist monk. But he honored his mother's request that he stay at home until his parents' death, to care for them in their old age.

In the following year, on Avalokiteshvara Bodhisattva's birthday, the Master dreamed that an old woman wearing a patchwork robe and a string of beads appeared to guide him through a wilderness in which he was lost. She radiated compassion as she led him over the road which was gutted with deep and dangerous holes. He knew that if he had tried to traverse this road alone, it would have been difficult, if not impossible, to reach safety; but as she guided him, the road became smooth and safe, and he could see clearly in all directions. Ahead was his home. Glancing back on the dangerous road, he saw many people following him—old and young, men and women, Sangha and scholars. "Who are these people?" he asked. "Where did they come from and where are they going?"

"They have affinities with you," she said, "and they also want to go home. You must guide them well and show them the Way so that all may arrive safely at Nirvana. I have important work to do elsewhere, and so I shall leave you now, but we shall soon meet again."

The Master asked her name and where she lived. "You will find out when you arrive home," she said. "There's no need to ask so many questions." Suddenly she whirled around and disappeared.

The Master led the people safely home and woke from his dream feeling extremely happy.

During that year he began bowing to his parents three times each, in the morning and in the evening, twelve bows a day. Then he thought, "The world is bigger than just my father and mother," and he began to bow to the heavens, to the earth, to the Emperor, and to his teachers as well. He bowed to his Master, although he had not yet met him. He bowed to the Buddhas, the Bodhisattvas, the Condition-Enlightened Ones, and the Arhats, and to all good people in the world, to thank them, on behalf of those they had helped, for all the good deeds they had done.

"Evil people are to be pitied," he thought, and he bowed for them, asking that their karmic offenses might be lessened and that they might learn to repent and reform. He thought of himself as the very worst of offenders. He thought of more and more people to bow for, until he was bowing eight hundred and thirty-seven times in the morning and eight hundred and thirty-seven times in the evening, about three hours a day in all.

The Master didn't let others see him bow. He rose at four in the morning, washed his face, went outside, lit a stick of incense, and bowed regardless of the weather. If there was snow on the ground, he bowed in the snow. In the evening, after everyone in the household had gone to bed, he went outside and bowed again. He kept up this practice daily for six years.

His filial devotion, which had become known far beyond his village, so that people referred to him as "Filial Son Bai," continued after his parents' deaths. When his mother was buried he remained beside her grave, where he sat in meditation for three years. The winter wind and rain and snow and ice and the hot summer sun found their way into the hut of sorghum-stalks that he built for himself. Clothed only in a rag robe, he ate one meal a day when food was offered him; if none was offered, he did not eat. He never lay down when he slept. Only once during his vigil did he leave the graveside, when he went to Three Conditions Temple at Ping Fang

Station south of Harbin to receive the Shramanera (novice) Precepts from the Great Master Chang Zhi.

At the side of his mother's grave, the Master read many sutras. When he first read the *Dharma Flower (Lotus) Sutra*, he jumped for joy. He knelt and recited it for seven days and seven nights, forgetting to sleep, forgetting to eat, until eventually blood flowed from his eyes and his vision dimmed. Then he read the *Shurangama Sutra*, thoroughly investigating the Great Samadhi and quietly contemplating it: the three stoppings, the three contemplations, neither moving nor still. The Master has said of this experience:

> *I began to obtain a single-minded and profound stillness, and to penetrate the noumenal state. When I read the Avatamsaka Sutra, the enlightenment became boundless in its scope, indescribable in its magnificence, unsurpassed in its loftiness, and ineffable in its clarity. National Master Ch'ing Liang said:*
>
> > *Opening and disclosing the mysterious and subtle,*
> > *Understanding and expanding the mind and its states,*
> > *Exhausting the principle while fathoming the nature,*
> > *Penetrating the result which includes the cause,*
> > *Deep, wide, and interfused,*
> > *Vast, great, and totally complete.*
>
> *It is certainly so! It is certainly so! At that time I could not put down the text, and I bowed to and recited the Great Sutra as if it were clothing from which one must not part or food which one could not do without for even a day. And I vowed to see myself to its vast circulation.*

When the Master's filial duties were completed, he went into seclusion in Amitabha Cave in the mountains east of his home village. There he delved deeply into dhyana meditation and practiced rigorous asceticism, eating only pine nuts and drinking spring water. The area bounded in wild beasts, but they never disturbed the Master. Wolves and bears behaved like house-pets, tigers stopped to listen to his teaching, and wild birds gathered to hear the wonderful Dharma.

After his stay in the mountains, the Master returned to Three Conditions Monastery where he worked tirelessly for the propagation of the Dharma and where he helped the Venerable Masters Chang Zhi and Chang Ren to greatly expand the monastery. During those years, he visited many of the local Buddhist monasteries, attended intensive meditation and recitation sessions, and walked many miles to listen to lectures on the sutras, in addition to lecturing on the sutras himself. He visited various non-Buddhist religious establishments and learned thoroughly about their beliefs.

In 1946, the Master made a pilgrimage to Pu Tuo Mountain, where he received the Complete Precepts of a Bhikshu in 1947. Then, in 1948, after three thousand miles of travel, he reached Nan Hua Monastery near Canton and bowed before the Venerable Master Hsu Yun, the Forty-Fourth Patriarch in the line of succession from Shakyamuni Buddha. At that first meeting, the Venerable Master Yun, who was then 109 years old, recognized the Master as a worthy vessel of the Dharma, one capable of its propagation, and he sealed and certified the Master's spiritual skill and transmitted to him the wonderful mind-to-mind seal of all Buddhas. Thus the Master became the forty-fifth generation in a line descending from Shakyamuni Buddha, the nineteenth generation in China from Bodhidharma, and the ninth generation of the Wei-yang lineage. The Venerable Yun later sent to the Master a document entitled "The Treasury of the Orthodox Dharma Eye: the Source of Buddhas and Patriarchs;" the document bears the seals of Yun-chu Monastery and of the Venerable Yun, and serves as public certification of the Dharma-transmission.

In 1950, the Master resigned his post of Director of the Nan Hua Institute for the Study of the Vinaya, at Nan Hua Monastery, and journeyed to Hong Kong. There he lived in a mountainside cave in the New Territories, until the large influx of Sangha members fleeing the mainland required his help in establishing new monasteries and temples. He himself established two temples and a lecture-hall and helped to bring about the construction of many others. He dwelt in Hong Kong for twelve years. During that time, thousands were influenced by his arduous cultivation and awesome manner to take refuge with the Triple Jewel, to cultivate the dharma-door of reciting the Buddha's name, and to support the propagation of the Buddhadharma. The Master sponsored the carving of many holy images and the printing of sutras, and he conducted meditation and recitation sessions and lectured on the Dharma. His Great Compassion Dharmas of healing continued to relieve the suffering of many.

In 1962, the Master carried the Buddha's Dharma farther west to the shores of America, where he took up residence in San Francisco, sat in meditation, and waited for past causes to ripen and bear their fruit. In the beginning of the year 1968, the Master declared that the flower of Buddhism would bloom that year with five petals. In June the Master began a 96-day dharma assembly on the *Shurangama Sutra*, and five of the American disciples attending left the home-life and became bhikshus and bhikshunis under the Master's guidance. During the ensuring decades, hundreds of people have left the home-life in America under the Master's guidance.

Since 1968, the Master has delivered complete commentaries on the *Heart Sutra, Vajra (Diamond) Sutra, Sixth Patriarch's Dharma-Jewel Platform Sutra, Amitabha Sutra, Sutra Of The Past Vows of Earth Store Bodhisattva, Great Compassion Heart Dharani Sutra, Dharma Flower (Lotus) Sutra, Sutra In Forty-Two Sections, Shramanera Vinaya*, and others. In June, 1971 he began and in October, 1979 he completed an eight-year lecture-series on the *Avatamsaka Sutra*, the sutra of the Dharma realm. These texts, together with the Master's commentaries, are being translated into English and other Western languages by the Buddhist Text Translation Society, sponsored by the Dharma Realm Buddhist

Association[1]. More than thirty volumes have already been published, and many others are in preparation.

In 1971, the Master established Gold Mountain Monastery in San Francisco as a place of practice of the orthodox Buddha-dharma. The Master has made a vow that wherever he goes, the Proper Dharma will prevail and the Dharma-Ending Age will not appear. The Gold Mountain Doctrine expresses the force of this vow:

Freezing, we do not scheme,
Starving, we do not beg.
Dying of poverty, we ask for nothing.
We accord with conditions, but do not change.
We do not change in according with conditions.
These are our three great principles.

We renounce our lives to do the Buddha's work.
We shape our lives to create the ability
To make revolution in the Sangha order.
In our actions we understand the principles,
So that our principles are revealed in our actions.
We carry out the pulse of the Patriarch's
    mind-to-mind seal.

In 1976, the Master established the City of Ten Thousand Buddhas, a 420-acre campus with sixty major buildings at Wonderful Enlightenment Mountain near Ukiah, California, 110 miles north of San Francisco. At the City of Ten Thousand Buddhas are Tathagata Monastery for monks and Great Joyous Giving House for nuns, the Hall of Ten Thousand Buddhas, and Dharma Realm Buddhist University, which was founded in 1977. Also at the City of Ten Thousand Buddhas are Instilling Virtue Elementary School, Cultivating Virtue Secondary School, and the City of Ten

---

[1.] formerly "Sino-American Buddhist Association".

Thousand Buddhas Acupuncture Clinic, and plans are made for a home for the aged, an Institute for the Study of Eastern and Western Medicine, a World Religions Center, and other social and educational services. The City offers all sincere students and cultivators a great variety of doors through which to enter into their own inherent wisdom in order to benefit themselves and all beings.

Already in America, thousands of people have taken refuge with the Triple Jewel and have bowed to the Master as their teacher. The Master has vowed that as long as a single one of his disciples has not become a Buddha, he will not become a Buddha. He will wait. Meanwhile he daily turns the Dharma Wheel and uses every opportunity to teach and transform living beings.

Ice in the sky
Snow on the ground.
Tiny creatures beyond number die in the cold
Or sleep in hibernation.
Contemplate in the midst of stillness;
Investigate in the midst of movement.
When you wrestle with dragons
*   and subdue tigers in constant sport,*
Ghosts cry and spirits wail,
*   in strange magical transformations.*
The meaning of what is truly real
*   is severed from words.*
It cannot be thought of.
You should go forward quickly.

With the great and the small destroyed,
With no inside and no outside,
Every mote of dust
Contains the entire Dharma Realm
Complete, whole, and perfectly fused,
Interpenetrating without obstruction.
With two clenched fists,

shatter the cover of empty space.
Swallow in one mouthful
the source of the ocean of Buddhalands.
With kindness and compassion rescue all,
Spare neither blood nor sweat,
And never pause to rest.

Venerable Master Hua

Guo Zhou Rounds

Bodhisattva Precepts Disciple
Member, Buddhist Text Translation Society

Introduction Two

The *Heart of Prajna Paramita Sutra* strikes the keynote of the philosophy of the Emptiness School of Mahayana Buddhism. Like the Sword of the Diamond King, it cuts through the veneer of the experienced world deep into the core of the True Mind—the Cosmic Consciousness—that lies behind everything phenomenal and noumenal in the universe.

As Mahayana Buddhism teaches, the phenomenal world, including everything animate and inanimate, is nothing else than an illusory projection of the True Mind, the moving spirit behind the operation of the universe, the transformation of the myriad things, and the transmigration of all species of life. To elucidate this point, we may compare the True Mind to the mental state of a person who is wide awake. Excessive mental activities, such as momentary impulses, instinctive desires, and streams of thought, then lull him into a wild dream in which he finds himself in a vast illusory space illuminated by the sun and moon and studded with myriad planets and stars. In such a way, the phenomenal world comes into existence from nowhere. The lands, waters, and all species of life, including his dream-body and dream-mind, appear to him as real and tangible as in real existence.

Deluded and puzzled, he is not aware that the illusory body and mind, and the universe as well, are a mirage conjured up by the excessive activity of his True Mind, his Buddha-Nature, which tends to duplicate itself in the form of projections, although it never undergoes any change by itself. The same is true of the moon, which is reflected clearly in innumerable bodies of water on the earth, although it is high up in the sky far beyond the reach of all waters.

Misled by the hallucinatory mirage, the dreamer mistakes the false for the real and contents himself with an endless transmigration in the six realms of existence within the framework of time and space.

Like a castle in the air, the illusory body and mind, together with the dreamer's environment, come from nowhere and therefore have no place to go, because they are dream-works when viewed from the standpoint of his True Mind. It follows that the life and death of all sentient beings, and the coalescence and dispersion of the universe, do not affect the True Mind or the Buddha-nature, because a wild dream does not add to or subtract anything from the dreamer, no matter whether he is awake or asleep. Therefore, the *Sutra of Complete Enlightenment* says: "Life and death as well as Nirvana are like the empty dreams of yesterday."

As the *Heart Sutra* relates, Avalokiteshvara Bodhisattva, through constant practice of the profound prajna paramita, has seen through life and the experienced world, which appear to him as insubstantial and unreal as the reflection of a flower in a mirror or the projection of the moon in water. The *Heart Sutra* says,

> *When Avalokiteshvara Bodhisattva was practicing the profound prajna paramita, he illuminated the five skandhas and saw that they are all empty, and he crossed beyond all suffering and difficulty.*

The "five skandhas" are nothing else than our mental and physical activities and reactions, which cause endless anxieties, distress, and troubles to the experiencer so long as he remains alive. Constant practice of profound prajna paramita develops transcendental wisdom in the experiencer, so that he is able to perceive everything in its totality. Then there is no distinction between the experiencer and the experienced, the phenomenal and the noumenal, matter and mind, form and emptiness. Thus the sutra says: "Shariputra, form does not differ from emptiness; emptiness does not differ from form. Form itself is emptiness; emptiness itself is form." Viewed from the standpoint of totality, a person's body and mind are actually various projections of his True Mind. Therefore, there is no sense in his attaching any importance to his physical and mental activities and reactions—the five skandhas which constitute the source of all worries and trouble. Having awakened to the futility of life, he is freed from all worldly worries and attachments, "thus crossing beyond all suffering and difficulty."

What is meant by "prajna paramita?" "Prajna" is often referred to as intuitive wisdom. Prajna awakened or realized is "paramita," which means "reaching the other shore." Intuitive wisdom transcends all the dialectics and analytical processes of reasoning, characteristic of our discriminating mind. Intuitive wisdom goes beyond the world of the senses and intellect, which are characterized by dualism, in the sense that where there is an observer there is something observed; where there is an experiencer there is something experienced; where there is a seer there is something seen. Intuitive wisdom is an integrating principle which perceives the whole instead of being distracted by the parts. It is by prajna that everything phenomenal and noumenal is observed from the standpoint of its totality, thus acquiring a new meaning. Hence the *Shurangama Sutra* says,

> On the tip of a hair there stands a magnificent monastery dedicated to the Buddha. While residing in a grain of dust, one is able to set the great Dharma Wheel in motion.

"The other shore," or "paramita," means the perfect peace of mind and spiritual freedom that is achieved when one's mentality transcends the world of relativities to identify itself with the ultimate reality—the totality in which all discriminations and distinctions between oneself and others, past, present, and the future, worldly and transcendental, saintly and earthly, life and death, mind and matter, construction and destruction, the absolute and the relative, the negative and the affirmative, ignorance and wisdom, and so forth are all eliminated. Thus the sutra says,

Therefore, in emptiness there is no form, feeling, cognition, formation, or consciousness; no eyes, ears, nose, tongue, or mind; no sights, sounds, smells, tastes, objects of touch, or dharmas; no field of the eyes, up to an including no field of mind consciousness.

This is the state of mind in which the experiencer is one with the experienced, thus enjoying perfect freedom from the obstruction of matter, mind, and dharmas. It is the state of mind of the Bodhisattva, the enlightened being who has only a short way to go before attaining the final goal of Buddhahood. Thus the sutra says,

The Bodhisattva, through reliance on prajna paramita, is unimpeded in his mind. Because there is no impediment, he is not afraid, and he leaves distorted dream-thinking far behind. Ultimately Nirvana!

Professor H. T. Lee

Buddhist Studies and Chinese Studies
Dharma Realm Buddhist University,
Member, Buddhist Text Translation Society

Introduction Three

The *Heart of Prajna Paramita Sutra, with Verses Without a Stand and Prose Commentary*, consists of three parts: the sutra text itself, the Venerable Master Hsuan Hua's verse explanation, and the Master's lectured commentary on the text and verses together.

The sutra is an essential summary of the Mahayana Buddhist teachings about emptiness and is widely recited and studied throughout the Buddhist world. The *Verses Without a Stand*, written by the Venerable Master in the early 1960's, consist of fifteen stanzas of eight lines each, in the standard seven-character unrhymed Buddhist verse-form. The Master lectured on both the sutra and the verses at Buddhist Lecture Hall in San Francisco from April 20 to July 27, 1969. He had lectured on them once before, when they were first written, but no recording or other record of those lectures had been made.

During the second occasion, the lectures were recorded on tape, from which I made a draft translation. I had already made a first translation of the verses, together with explanatory notes, during 1968 and early 1969 an M.A. thesis in the Department of Asian Languages at the University of Washington. The translations of the sutra, verses, and lectured commentary, and extensive notes, were serially published in *Vajra Bodhi Sea*, nos. 8-25, between November, 1970 and April, 1972.

I was subsequently unable to work further on the translation until 1977, when I was able to extensively revise the verse translation and to work further on the translation of the sutra and the spoken commentary. The entire work was then edited by Upasaka Guo Zhou (David) Rounds, who has done much to enhance its readability and clarity.

The Chinese text of the spoken commentary was transcribed from the original tapes by my wife, Upasika Guo Han (Yao Sen Liu Epstein), and was published in 1979, together with the Chinese text of the sutra and the verses, by the Buddhist Text Translation Society, as a companion volume to the present one. Since the Chinese transcription and the English translation were edited independently, they do not always coincide exactly. Nevertheless, I am confident they do not differ in any important aspect.

What for me is most outstanding about the *Verses Without a Stand and Prose Commentary* is its direct and practical approach. Therefore, since the translation is intended primarily for those who wish to put it to use, we have not encumbered the text with technical apparatus of interest only to the scholar. Notes are limited to explanatory references and no attempt has been made to refer the reader to the scholarly literature. Sanskrit is given where it may be of special interest. Where Sanskrit and English are not entirely equivalent, the English has been translated from the Chinese and the Sanskrit has been given as reference.

Since the verses are both profound and terse, it is difficult to convey their full meaning in English. In the translation I have striven to communicate clearly the simplest levels of understanding and have made no attempt to reproduce the poetic qualities of the verses. Hopefully, in the future someone of greater skill and sensitivity will be able to render into English more fully their magnificent beauty.

A final word about the process of translation: as with all translation done under the auspices of the Buddhist Text Translation Society, the present work has been reviewed, edited, and certified by highly qualified people, all of whom adhere to the Society's Rules for Translators, which are listed in this book.

Upasaka Kuo-jung (R.B.) Epstein

Vice-President and Dean of Letters and Science
Dharma Realm Buddhist University
Member, Buddhist Text Translation Society

Eight Guidelines of BTTS

1. A volunteer must free him/herself from the motives of personal fame and profit.
2. A volunteer must cultivate a respectful and sincere attitude free from arrogance and conceit.
3. A volunteer must refrain from aggrandizing his/her work and denigrating that of others.
4. A volunteer must not establish him/herself as the standard of correctness and suppress the work of others with his or her fault-finding.
5. A volunteer must take the Buddha-mind as his/her own mind.
6. A volunteer must use the wisdom of Dharma-Selecting Vision to determine true principles.
7. A volunteer must request Virtuous Elders in the ten directions to certify his/her translations.
8. A volunteer must endeavour to propagate the teachings by printing Sutras, Shastra texts, and Vinaya texts when the translations are certified as being correct.

釋迦牟尼文佛

Namo Original Teacher Shakyamuni Buddha

Verse for Opening a Sutra

The unsurpassed, profound, and wonderful dharma,
Is difficult to encounter in hundreds of millions of eons,
I now see and hear it, receive and uphold it,
And I vow to fathom the Tathagata's true meaning.

PART I

THE HEART OF PRAJNA PARAMITA SUTRA

When Avalokiteshvara Bodhisattva was practicing the profound prajna paramita, he illuminated the five skandhas and saw that they are all empty, and he crossed beyond all suffering and difficulty.

Shariputra, form does not differ from emptiness; emptiness does not differ from form. Form itself is emptiness; emptiness itself is form. So, too, are feeling, cognition, formation, and consciousness.

Shariputra, all dharmas are empty of characteristics. They are not produced. Not destroyed, not defiled, not pure, and they neither increase nor diminish. Therefore, in emptiness there is no form, feeling, cognition, formation, or consciousness; no eyes, ears, nose, tongue, body, or mind; no sights, sounds, smells, tastes, objects of touch, or dharmas; no field of the eyes, up to and including no field of mind-consciousness; and no ignorance or ending of ignorance, up to and including no old age and death or ending of old age and death. There is no suffering, no accumulating, no extinction, no Way, and no understanding and no attaining.

Because nothing is attained, the Bodhisattva, through reliance on prajna paramita, is unimpeded in his mind. Because there is no impediment, he is not afraid, and he leaves distorted dream-thinking far behind. Ultimately Nirvana!

All Buddhas of the three periods of time attain Anuttarasamyaksambodhi through reliance on prajna paramita. Therefore, know that prajna paramita is a great spiritual mantra, a great bright mantra, a supreme mantra, an unequalled mantra. It can remove all suffering; it is genuine and not false. That is why the mantra of prajna paramita was spoken. Recite it like this:

Gate gate paragate parasamgate bodhi svaha!

PART II

A GENERAL EXPLANATION OF THE TITLE

Commentary:

The explanation of the *Heart Sutra* will be divided into two sections: a general explanation of the title, and an explanation of the meaning of the text. The general explanation of the title will be further divided into a discussion of the sutra title and a discussion of the translator.

Seven categories of titles have been divised for the three treasuries (*tripitaka*) and the twelve divisions of the sutras spoken by the Buddha:

1) The first kind of title refers exclusively to persons. The *Buddha Speaks of Amitabha Sutra* is an example, since both Shakyamuni Buddha and Amitabha Buddha are personages.

2) The *Nirvana Sutra* is an example of a title which is determined exclusively by reference to dharma. Nirvana, which signifies a dharma (*dharmalaksana*), is used for its title.

3) In the third category are titles comprised of analogies. The *Brahma Net Sutra* is an example of this kind of title. The text of the sutra employs in its discussion of the precepts (the rules of moral conduct taught by the Buddha) the analogy of the cylindrical net-curtain belonging to the king of the Great Brahma Heaven; the

curtain is a manifestation of his adornments. All through the net-curtain are holes, and in the empty space of each hole there is a precious pearl, each the brightest and most valuable of all pearls. All the way around, the precious pearls illuminate each other with light, and the emptiness interpenetrates. This precious pearl illuminates that precious pearl – back and forth. That is what is meant by their "illuminating each other."

Your light illuminates my light and my light illuminates yours. However, the lights do not oppose one another. One of them is incapable of saying, "Keep your light out of my light," or, "I don't want my light to shine on you." There is none of that; they illuminate each other and the emptiness interpenetrates.

In other words, then, the precepts are like the light of the precious pearls; they illuminate each other. If you keep a precept, that is, if you obey a rule of moral conduct without fail, it emits light. Each precept you keep has light. Each of the ten major and forty-eight minor Bodhisattva precepts, which are explained in the *Brahma Net Sutra* emits rays of light, just like the pearls in the Brahma net-curtain.

Why are the precious pearls embroidered in the holes? It indicates to us that originally, before we keep the Bodhisattva precepts, there are holes. How do we know there are holes? Because there are leaks, also called outflows (*asrava*). Yet the leaks can be transformed into precious pearls. If you keep a precept, a precious pearl shines. If you break a precept, there is a leak. "The lights illuminate each other and the emptiness interpenetrates" represents the Buddhadharma, the minds of the Buddhas, the minds of the Bodhisattvas, and the minds of all living beings – every mind responding to every other, mind with mind.

How did the Buddhas realize Buddhahood? It was through the cultivation of the precepts. And Bodhisattvas as well must cultivate the precepts to become Buddhas. Living beings must also keep the precepts; then they can cultivate and become Buddhas. All this represents transformation, endless transformation. Thus the title of the *Brahma Net Sutra* is comprised exclusively of analogy.

The first three of the seven kinds of sutra titles are called the unitary three, while the next three kinds are called the dual three:

4) The first of the three kinds of dual title makes reference to both persons and dharmas. The *Manjushri Asks about Prajna Sutra* is an example, since Manjushri is a person and prajna is a particular dharma.

5) The next kind of title refers to both persons and analogies; the *Lion's Roar of the Thus Come One Sutra* is an example. The Thus Come One (*tathagata*) is a person, and the lion's roar is an analogy. The Buddha's exclamation of the Dharma is likened to a lion's roar: "When the lion roars, the hundred beasts are terrified."

6) The sixth kind of title is established by reference to dharma and analogy. In the *Heart of Prajna Paramita Sutra*, prajna paramita is the dharma and heart is the analogy.

7) The one remaining variation combines all three unitary elements: person, dharma, and analogy. The *Sutra of the Flowering Adornment of the Buddha of Great Expanse*, commonly known as the *Avatamsaka Sutra*, is the example here. This kind of title is said to be "complete in one." Great Expanse symbolizes the substance of the dharma, and Flowering Adornment represents its function. The dharma of great expanse was cultivated by the Buddha in order to realize Buddhahood. He cultivated the six paramitas and the ten thousand practices and used the flowering of those causes to adorn the attainment of the supreme fruit, which is Buddhahood.

The Five Categories of Recondite Meaning

Now I will explain the text of the sutra by means of eight-line verses, which I wrote some time ago. I used them once before to lecture on this sutra. This is the first verse:

Verse:

> *Wonderful wisdom can reach the other shore*
> > *right now;*
> *The true mind itself can merge with*
> > *enlightenment's source.*
> *Dharma and analogy comprise its title,*
> > *which transcends the relative.*
> *Empty of the characteristics of all dharmas*
> > *is this substance beyond words.*
> *Fundamental non-attainment is its purpose*
> > *and intent,*
> *And by using its power of eradication,*
> > *the three obstacles are cleansed away.*
> *The "butter division" is determined to be*
> > *the meaning of this teaching,*
> *A maha turning around:*
> > *this is the prajna boat.*

Commentary:

Each of the eight lines of the first verse speaks about the *Heart of Prajna Paramita Sutra* according to the five categories of recondite meaning.

1) Explanation of the Title. The first three lines of the verse explain the meaning of the title of the sutra in accordance with the first category of recondite meaning, the explanation of the title.

Wonderful wisdom can reach the other shore right now. Prajna is wonderful wisdom, and paramita means to reach the other shore. When you use the wonderful wisdom of prajna, you reach the other shore.

The true mind itself can merge with enlightenment's source. To say "true mind" is to speak both of the mind and of prajna. When you have the wonderful wisdom of prajna, you have the true mind, and so you naturally merge with the source of enlightenment. You are united with the original enlightenment of the Buddha; you join with it; you flow into and become the substance of the original enlightenment. "Merge" implies uniting into a single substance.

Dharma and analogy comprise its title, which transcends the relative. The title, the *Heart of Prajna Paramita Sutra*, is made up of references to both dharma and analogy. The phrase "which transcends the relative" indicates a dharma which reaches a state of non-relativity. Prajna paramita is that dharma, and heart is the analogy.

There are three types of prajna: the prajna of language, the prajna of contemplative illumination, and the prajna of the characteristic of actuality. The prajna of the characteristic of actuality is the ultimate wisdom, wonderful wisdom, and the wisdom which penetrates to the foundation. It can also be said to be the wisdom which arrives home and the wisdom of the Buddha.

What else can it be called? It is called the true heart[1]. The true heart is wisdom; wisdom is the true heart. Because prajna can be translated as "true heart," the two hundred fifty or so words of this sutra are the heart within the heart – the heart within the six hundred chapters of the prajna text of the *Great Prajna Sutra*. Yet in still another way it is the heart within the heart. The sutra is the heart of prajna, and since prajna is the heart, it is the heart of that heart. And therefore the text is called the *Heart Sutra*. Since prajna can be translated as heart or mind, the *Great Prajna Sutra* can be called the *Great True Heart Sutra*. It's not a false heart – not a false mind. The present sutra explains fully the wonderful principle of its actual use.

The dharma in the title is prajna paramita, the dharma of reaching the other shore. "Heart" is the analogy, and it is used in the sutra to indicate that the heart (which is to say the mind) is the theme of one's entire life and that it transcends all opposites.

2) Discernment of the Substance. *Empty of the characteristics of all dharmas is this substance beyond words.* What is the sutra's substance? It is "empty of the characteristics of all dharmas," a phrase which is different in wording but identical in meaning to the line in the sutra text, "All dharmas are empty of characteristics." "Empty of characteristics" simply means that the substance of the sutra is without any characteristics, and "substance beyond words" means that nothing can be said about it. Since its substance is "empty of the characteristics of all dharmas," there isn't anything at all. You ask, "Then what is there that is worth saying?" This "substance beyond words" has already passed beyond the characteristics of speech, the characteristics grasped by the mind, the characteristics of written language; it has passed beyond all characteristics. It is all dharmas.

3) Elucidation of its basic purpose. *Fundamental non-attainment is its purpose and intent.* The fifth line of verse explains the third recondite meaning, elucidation of the sutra's

---

1. In Chinese, the character *xin* 心 means both heart and mind. The word "heart" in the Sanskrit title of the sutra is translated as *hrdaya*. The usual Sanskrit word for mind or heart in the non-physical sense is *citta*. The Chinese character *xin* is used as a translation for both *hrdaya* and *citta*.

basic purpose: fundamental non-attainment. In one passage the sutra says, **"There is… no understanding and no attaining."** Non-attainment is the sutra's purpose and intent.

Now I will make use of worldly dharmas to explain the Buddha-dharma. The word "person" is an ordinary noun, the designation by which human beings are distinguished from other categories. Just as a person is simply called a person, analogously every sutra is called a sutra. Now what is a certain person's specific name? The name by which he is identified is perhaps Smith or Brown. To discuss the specific name is what is meant by explanation of the title. What does Smith look like? Is he tall or short, black or white, fat or thin? What about his body[2]? Is it fully formed or not? Does he have eyes? Ears? A nose? That is what is meant by investigating the characteristics of his substance.

After the substance has been revealed, then the basic purpose should be elucidated. What is meant by elucidation of the basic purpose? Smith is very learned he could be a secretary or a Ph.D. That is what is meant.

4) Discussion of the Function. Continuing the analogy, what does Smith do all day? What can he do? Observations of that sort reveal the person's usefulness and capabilities.

And by using its power of eradication, the three obstacles are cleansed away. "Eradication" is what the sutra is capable of doing. What can the *Heart of Prajna Paramita Sutra* do? Its function is to cleanse away the three obstacles: the retribution-obstacle, the activity-obstacle, and the affliction-obstacle.

Of retribution-obstacles, the first of the three obstacles, there are two kinds: dependent retribution and primary retribution[3]. Primary retribution is the body, while dependent retribution refers to food, clothing, dwelling, and so forth – the material environment on which the body is dependent. Therefore, primary retribution is

---

[2.] In Chinese the single character *ti* 體 means both body and substance.

[3.] In Chinese, the character *bao* 報 means both reward and retribution.

the retribution you are undergoing right now, the dependent retribution is your environment.

There are all sorts of primary retribution. Some bodies are good ones and some are not. Some are especially full and handsome in their appearance, so that everyone who sees them likes them. Merely by looking upon a particular body, everyone loves and respects the person as someone who is outstanding.

Perhaps a particular person really has wisdom, or another really has good roots. With respect to good roots and wisdom there are two types of people. First are those who have wisdom and no good roots. What are those people like? Most of them are weird ghosts and monstrous demons who have come into the world as people. They were mountain essences who after a long time as old spirits and ghosts became capable of eating people, and when they died, they were able to be reborn as people possessed of a little bit of intelligence. Compared to most people they are intelligent, but they muddle up everything they do – their activities are not at all intelligent. They do whatever is harmful, and, without exception, they lack propriety. Everything that is most harmful to people and disruptive to the order of society is what they want to do. Such people, the ones who have some wisdom but no good roots, seem only to be afraid that the world won't be in disorder.

The second kind, those who have good roots but no wisdom, are those who in their lives exclusively performed good deeds but did not study the sutras. As a consequence they don't have much wisdom; in fact, they are very stupid.

Some people undergo the primary retribution of being especially ugly. Others have both a beautiful and full appearance and a long life full of wealth, honor, and respect. Still others have a very short life besides being ugly. There are all kinds of primary retributions, which are the fruitions of causes planted in the past.

Dependent retribution consists of one's living conditions, clothes, food, and so forth. It too comes from causes in your previous lives. If in previous lives you planted seeds of good, the fruition in this life will be a good reward. If in former lives you planted the seeds of evil, they will reveal themselves in this life by their fruition in your retribution. Therefore, you should certainly be very cautious in everything you do! If you do not plant the causes of evil, then in the future you won't undergo their fruition in evil retribution.

The second of the three obstacles is the activity-obstacle. Not only those who have left the home-life to become members of the Sangha[4], but also those at home should certainly have an occupational activity. While involved in a particular activity, many problems will arise, many difficult situations which will make you afflicted and unhappy. That is what is meant by the activity-obstacle.

The third obstacle is the affliction-obstacle. Everybody has afflictions, yet where do they come from? Most are generated from thoughts of greed, of anger, and of stupidity. How can you acquire afflictions? Have greed in your mind, insatiable greed, and afflictions will arise. How else can you acquire afflictions? Have a temper. A situation isn't right for you, and so you become afflicted with anger. Again, how do you give rise to afflictions? By being stupid. You misunderstand situations and so are afflicted.

Why do you become afflicted? Thoughts of contempt, of arrogance, and of condescension generate afflictions. Furthermore, you doubt everything, and because of your doubting you become afflicted.

Why are you still afflicted right now? Because you have deviant views and see situations incorrectly. If no matter what is happening, you have proper knowledge, proper views, and genuine wisdom, you will see very, very clearly and will understand completely. When clarity and understanding appear in the midst of circumstances, then there is no affliction. It is the deviant views of

---

[4.] The Sangha is the community of Buddhist bhikshus (monks) and bhikshunis (nuns).

greed, hatred, stupidity, arrogance, and doubt that produce the affliction-obstacle.

The *Heart Sutra* can remove the three obstacles: the retribution-obstacle, the activity-obstacle, and the affliction-obstacle. How? It contains the genuine, wonderful wisdom which is the unmoving mind of true suchness, and so it removes and destroys the three obstacles. Wonderful wisdom: if we understand the *Heart of Prajna Paramita Sutra*, then we can have that genuine wisdom; and with genuine wisdom, we can remove and destroy the three obstacles.

5) Determination of the Characteristics of the Teaching. The fifth recondite meaning is described by the seventh line of the verse. The *"butter division"*[5] *is determined to be the meaning of this teaching.* The prajna paramita sutras belong to the "butter division." "Butter" represents the fourth or prajna period of the five periods of the Buddha's teaching.

A Maha turning around: this is the prajna-boat. Maha is the Sanskrit word for "great." To turn the prajna-boat around doesn't mean to turn it over. If you turn it over, there isn't any prajna. You should turn your stupidity around, and that will be the prajna-boat; that is prajna. It can be compared to moving a boat up-stream. It is necessary to use a little effort, and it is not something that can be

---

5. The "butter-division" refers to the milk-products analogy for the periods of the Buddha's teaching. The analogy is found in the *Mahaparinirvana Sutra* and was used by the Tian Tai School in conjunction with the five periods of the Buddha's teaching. In the analogy, the original Dharma-nourishment is taken to be fresh milk. In each successive period it becomes richer and more purified. Yet it is all the same basic substance, the source-nourishment. Butter represents the prajna teachings of the fourth period, to which the *Heart Sutra* belongs. The five periods of the Buddha's teaching and the milk-products analogy are these:

1. *Avatamsaka* (21 days) whole milk (*ksira*)
2. *Agama* or *Mrgadava* (12 years) coagulated milk (*dadhi*)
3. *Vaipulya* (8 years) curds (*nevanita*)
4. *Prajna-paramita* (22 years) butter (*ghrta*)
5. *Saddharmapundarika-Mahaparinirvana* (8 years) clarified butter (*ghee*)

done easily. Although you don't need to take three great asamkhyeya kalpas – three incalculably long ages – you must pass through at least one or two or perhaps three lifetimes before you can attain genuine wisdom.

"Oh," you say, "even though it doesn't require kalpas, it's still a really long time, so I'm not going to cultivate."

If you don't want to cultivate, it's not necessary; certainly no one will force you. Forcing is not the Way. Where my own disciples are concerned, I allow anyone who wants to fall to fall according to his own inclinations. If you don't want to turn the prajna boat around, then you can follow the great flow, flow along with the current, and go downstream, go farther and farther down. If you turn around, you move upstream, and if you don't turn around, you flow downstream. Take a look. Are you going upstream or downstream?

The Five Periods of the Buddha's Teaching

The Dharma spoken by the Buddhas was divided into five periods and eight teachings by the Great Master Zhi Yi, "The Wise One" (538-597 A.D.). The five periods will be categorized by means of the two kinds of wisdom, expedient and actual.

1) The *Avatamsaka* period represented in the world by the *Avatamsaka Sutra*, consists in the Dharma spoken by the Buddha during the first twenty-one days of his teaching. The period includes one kind of expedient Dharma and one kind of actual Dharma: the gradual and the sudden. That is, the *Avatamsaka Sutra* teaches one kind of expedient wisdom and one kind of actual wisdom. The *Avatamsaka Sutra* explains the doctrine of the dharma realms: the dharma realm of phenomena; the noumenal dharma realm; the dharma realm in which phenomena are unobstructed; the dharma realm in which noumenon is unobstructed; and the dharma realm in which both phenomena and noumenon are unobstructed. Although this teaching was spoken for the sake of Bodhisattvas, the *Avatamsaka Sutra* nonetheless contains one kind of expedient dharma, along with the actual wisdom, that is, along with the real Buddhadharma.

2) In the second or *Agama* period, the Buddha spoke no actual Dharma, or actual wisdom, but instead spoke an expedient Dharma. At that time all sentient beings were like children, and since they did not understand the Buddhadharma, the Buddha used various

expedient dharma-doors to induce and guide them, to transform them, and to take them across.

3) During the third period, the *Vaipulya*, the Buddha spoke three kinds of expedient Dharma and one kind of actual Dharma. At that time the four teachings were explained together: the treasury (*tripitaka*) teaching of the Hinayana; the connecting teaching; and the special teaching, which are the three expedient dharmas; and the perfect teaching, which is actual Dharma. "Revile the one-sided and upbraid the small" indicates that the one-sidedness of the small vehicle, the Hinayana, is wrong. "Praise the great and extol the perfect" commends the perfect teaching of the great vehicle, the Mahayana. In the Vaipulya period, the four teachings were explained together.

4) The fourth period is the *Prajna* period. In it there were two kinds of expedient Dharma – the connecting and special teachings – and one kind of actual Dharma, the perfect teaching.

5) In the *Lotus-Nirvana* period, which includes the *Wonderful Dharma Lotus Flower Sutra* and the *Mahaparinirvana Sutra*, there was no expedient Dharma; there was only actual Dharma and actual wisdom.

To summarize the five periods, in the Lotus-Nirvana period, only actual Dharma appears; there is no expedient Dharma. In the Prajna period, two expedient dharmas and one actual Dharma appear. In the Vaipulya period, three expedients and one actual Dharma appear. In the Agama period there is only expedient and no actual Dharma, and in the Avatamsaka period there is one expedient and one actual – the gradual and the sudden. The above explanation employs the two types of wisdom, expedient and actual, to categorize the five periods. If the periods were explained in detail, there would be much, much more to say.

So in lecturing on the sutras I explain a little more each time, I tell you a little more of what you haven't heard. Listen a lot and you will understand a lot.

The Meaning of "Sutra"

Sutras have both a generic and a specific title. The generic title is simply "Sutra," while the specific title distinguishes one sutra from another. The *Heart of Prajna Paramita Sutra* is the specific title of this sutra. "Prajna Paramita" is the dharma, "Heart" is the analogy, "Sutra" is the sutra. The *Heart of Prajna Paramita* is the heart within the heart. No other sutra in the Prajna Division has this name. I have already explained the specific title, the *Heart of Prajna Paramita*, by an eight-line verse. Now the word "Sutra" will be fully explained.

What is a sutra? A sutra is defined as "path", the path necessarily passed through in cultivation of the Way. If you wish to cultivate, you must move along that path; if you don't want to cultivate, following it is unnecessary. But, if you do want to cultivate, "Sutra" is the path you must take. Now, if people don't walk on a path, it becomes wild and overgrown with vegetation. For example, you may have been able to recite the *Heart of Prajna Paramita Sutra* without referring to a text, but then four or five months pass without your reciting it, and you forget it. That forgetting is the path becoming overgrown. However, if you walk the path, if you cultivate the Way, then it won't become overgrown, but every day will become smoother and brighter.

What is the benefit of reciting sutras? Reciting sutras doesn't yield any benefits. You waste a lot of time and use a lot of energy to recite a sutra. For instance, what is gained by reciting the *Heart*

Sutra in front of the Buddha? You read it from beginning to end, waste energy, spirit, and time, but don't see any return from it. Ah, cultivators, don't be so stupid! The benefits which you can see are not real; all appearances are empty and false. To grasp at a form, at what you can see, is not a benefit. That is why reciting sutras isn't beneficial.

Don't search for benefits. Recite the sutra once and your own nature is cleaned once. When you recite the *Heart Sutra* once, you have the feeling that you understand a little of its meaning; recite it twice or three times, and each time you understand a little more. Reciting sutras helps the wisdom of your own nature to grow. How much? You can't see it; nevertheless, you can have a kind of feeling about it. Therefore, it is not possible to talk about the benefits of reciting sutras.

Moreover, each time you recite the sutra your afflictions decrease. You shouldn't get upset during recitation by thinking, "You over there, you recited it wrong. You recited it too fast; I can't keep up with you. The sounds that you make when you recite are really unpleasant, so I don't like to listen to it." No, don't waste your effort in those directions. When reciting sutras or mantras, everyone should chant together. It isn't necessary for everyone to know the language the sutra is being recited in; but able to read the sutra or not, everyone should recite along together. For everyone to practice together, though, doesn't mean your looking for my faults, and my looking for your faults. If there are really faults, everyone should find them. And if you yourself don't find your own faults because they are too big, then your cultivation will not be attuned to receive a response.

Reciting sutras is a great help to one's own nature in developing wisdom. Reciting the *Diamond Sutra* develops wisdom; reciting the *Heart Sutra* develops even more wisdom. You say that there aren't any benefits gained from reciting sutras, yet the benefits are very great. It's just that you don't see them. You don't see them? Then they are real benefits. Anything that you can see is just the skin.

The word "sutra" has four other meanings: that which strings together; that which attracts; that which is permanent; and a method. "Stringing together" refers to the connecting of all the meanings which were spoken to make a sutra, as if a piece of thread were used to string them together.

A sutra "attracts" in that it can make use of opportunities for the transformation of sentient beings. This particular sutra is capable of responding to the causal opportunities of all sentient beings and of giving each a medicine to cure that being's own particular disease. Just as a strong magnet can attract iron from a great distance, a sutra, like a magnet, draws in all sentient beings. We sentient beings are like iron, hard and stubborn, with large tempers and many faults. But as soon as we are pulled into the magnet, we begin to be slowly softened so that our faults fall away. That is the meaning of "that which attracts".

A sutra is "permanent" because it is eternally unchanging dharma, and has neither beginning nor end. Not one word can be omitted from or added to a sutra; thus it is eternal. In ancient times and in the present, living beings have cultivated and will continue to cultivate according to this sutra.

A sutra is a "method" followed in cultivation of the Way. In the three periods of time, past, present, and future, one cultivates according to this Dharma. What is honored in the three periods of time alike is called the method. What is unchanging in the past and present is called the permanent.

Sutra also has the meaning of a marking-line. In ancient China carpenters used a tool called the ink-cup and line. It consisted of a string which was inked black. When the carpenters wanted to be sure that their construction was straight and true, they would stretch the string out, pull it back, and snap it to, in order to make a straight black guideline.

To sum up, a sutra is a set of rules. To recite sutras is to follow the rules. If you don't recite sutras, then you don't follow the rules.

Since you are now studying prajna, you certainly should respect the rules of prajna. If you do, you will certainly develop your wisdom.

I have spoken in general about the title of the sutra, and now I will talk about the translator. For everything we understand of this sutra, we should give great thanks to the translator. If he had never existed, we should be unable to see the sutra or even to hear its name. If that were the case, how would we be able to cultivate according to the methods prescribed in it? It would be impossible to find its path of cultivation. Therefore, we should thank the person who translated the sutra, since from that time up to the present moment, every generation has benefited from his compassionate teaching and transforming. It follows that the merit derived from translating sutras is inconceivably great.

The Translator

The text says that the *Heart of Prajna Paramita Sutra* was **translated by Tang Dharma Master of the Tripitaka Hsüan-Tsang on imperial command.**

Tang refers to the Tang Dynasty of China (618-907 A.D.). **Tripitaka** is Sanskrit for "three storehouses" – the three storehouses of the Buddhist Canon. They are the *sutras*, which teach samadhi[6], the *vinaya*, which contains the precepts, or rules of moral conduct, and the *shastras*, which contain discussions of doctrine. A **Dharma Master** is one who takes the Buddhadharma as his master and also one who uses the Buddhadharma to teach and transform living beings. This Dharma Master, **Hsüan-Tsang**, took the Dharma as his master, and he also used it to transform sentient beings. He was perfect on both counts, so either way you use the title Dharma Master, it applies to him.

Dharma Master Hsüan Tsang's roots were especially deep, thick, and wonderful. The state of his existence was inconceivable. From his own time up to the present he is Buddhism's greatest Dharma Master. One might ask, "How can you say that he is the greatest?" When he went to India during the Tang Dynasty to bring back the texts of sutras to China, the great modern transportation network of buses, planes, boats, and trains did not exist. What did Dharma Master Hsüan Tsang use for transportation? He went from

---

6. Single-minded concentration

China through Siberia across the Himalayas to India on horseback. Such a journey is extremely long and involves much suffering, for no others had made the trip before him. Even though there were no mountains where he lived, Tang Master Hsüan Tsang, before he left to bring back the sutras, practiced running and mountain-climbing every day. How did he do it? He piled up a lot of chairs and tables and jumped from one to the next, from table to chair back and forth. By practicing at home before undertaking the extremely long journey, he was able to attain his aim and reach India. He lived there for fourteen years and collected many sutras which he brought back to China.

When he returned from India, he received an **imperial command** to translate the sutras into Chinese from their original language of India. Now it is up to you Westerners to translate the sutras into the languages of the West. The merit derived by the people who take part in this work will be without limit, for it will benefit not only their own lives, but will be cause for the gratitude of generations of people in the West. Everyone can be included in the work of translation; no one should fall behind in learning Chinese. You Westerners should make an offering to the people of the West.

Now it can be said that the world has gone bad. Only if people understand the Buddhadharma can the evil age be turned back. If people don't understand the Buddhadharma, then I am afraid this world will arrive at the time when it will be destroyed. The Christians talk about Judgment Day – the Last Day. If the Buddhadharma is translated into English, if everyone understands the Buddhadharma, if everyone knows better than to be lazy, and if people come forward to cultivate the Way with open hearts and minds, then the Last Day will be very far away in the future; it will be hard to say how many great ages away.

Basically there isn't any "Last Day". Why? Because the turning of the great Dharma wheel of the Buddhadharma will even pull in the sun, which then will be unable to set on a Last Day. There won't be any final day. All such matters are living; they're not fixed, certain, and dead. Don't think that what is called the Last Day is the Last Day, for then there will in fact be a final day. Now, which is more probable: that there will be a final day or won't be one? If everyone studies the Buddhadharma, then the day of destruction won't come. It's all very alive, so don't see it as fixed and dead.

For instance, from time to time people have spread the rumor that there is going to be an earthquake in San Francisco that will cause it to fall into the sea. For several years now people have been talking about this, and a lot of wealthy people who are afraid of dying have moved away.

I spoke about this last year, too, and at that time one of my disciples in San Francisco sent another disciple in Seattle a letter saying that I couldn't go to Seattle, because if I did, San Francisco would fall into the sea. I was unable to buy a plane ticket, and even though they were going to give me a plane ticket, I couldn't go. At that time I told everyone, "If you really study the Buddhadharma, San Francisco won't be allowed to move, because I haven't lived here long enough." Why did I say that? Well, this year I said to everyone, "Relax, all you have to do is recite the *Shurangama Mantra* and study the Buddhadharma with a sincere mind, and I will guarantee that San Francisco won't budge." I said that.

Why hasn't San Francisco moved up till now? Because there are some people who have changed a little. Everybody recites the *Shurangama Mantra* and studies the Buddhadharma with a very sincere mind, so the gods, dragons, and the rest of the eightfold division of gods and ghosts are here to protect our *Bodhimanda*[7], our place of cultivation, to see that there are no disruptions. The meaning is the same as for the Last Day. If it is possible for the Last Day not to be the Last Day, it is even more possible that San Francisco won't move, even if it wants to. It can't find some other suitable place to rent, and it already has such a good place that it isn't moving.

[7.] Way place, platform or seat of enlightenment. Chinese *dao chang* 道場, a place for cultivation.

PART III

EXPLANATION OF THE MEANING OF THE TEXT

Sutra:

When Avalokiteshvara Bodhisattva

Verse:

> *Reversing the light to shine within,*
> *Avalokiteshvara enlightens all the sentient beings;*
> *   thus he is a Bodhisattva.*
> *His mind is thus, thus, unmoving,*
> *   a superior one at peace;*
> *With total understanding of the ever-shining,*
> *   he is host and master.*
> *Six types of psychic powers are an ordinary matter,*
> *And even less can the winds and rains*
> *   of the eight directions cause alarm.*
> *He rolls it up and secretly hides it away;*
> *And lets it go to fill the entire world.*

Commentary:

The name *Avalokiteshvara* is Sanskrit; in Chinese it is rendered *guan zi zai* 觀自在, "Contemplating Ease". To be at ease is to be happy about everything and to be without worries or obstacles. To be unimpeded is to contemplate ease. If you are impeded, then you are not contemplating ease. *Reversing the light to shine within* is contemplating ease. If you don't reverse the light to shine within, you're not contemplating ease.

What is meant by "reversing the light to shine within"? Regardless of what the situation is, examine yourself. If someone has wronged you, you should think to yourself, "Basically, I was wrong."

If you say, "When people don't act properly toward me, I don't look to see whether I'm right myself; I just smash them right away, smash their heads in so that blood flows" – then you haven't won a victory, but have only shown your complete lack of principles and wisdom. To reverse the light to shine within is to have principles and wisdom. Reverse the light and contemplate whether or not you are at ease.

I will explain the two characters *zi zai* 自在, which together mean "ease". The *zi* is oneself, and the *zai* is where one is. I'll say it word for word. Are you right here (*zai*), or aren't you? In other words, do you have false thoughts, or not? If one has false thoughts, then one (*zi*) is not right here. It's very simple. To reverse the light to shine within is simply to see whether you have false thoughts. If you have false thoughts, then you aren't at ease. If you don't have false thoughts, then you are at ease. That's how wonderful it is.

Avalokiteshvara enlightens all the sentient beings; thus he is a Bodhisattva. What is a Bodhisattva? A Bodhisattva is somebody who wants to enlighten sentient beings. The Chinese word for "enlighten" is *jiao* 覺, to make people understand. It isn't the *jiao* 攪, which means to stir up trouble. Add the element "hand" 扌 to the character *jiao* 覺, meaning to enlighten, and it becomes another *jiao* 攪: it turns into a lot of trouble. The stirring-up-trouble *jiao* is not to enlighten sentient beings, but to make them stupid and to try to turn what is good in their lives into what is evil.

But here in the verse, *jiao* means to bring understanding to all sentient beings.

What is meant by "sentient?" Be careful not to misunderstand the text here by hastily assuming that the word "sentient" (*you qing* 有情) means emotional love (*qing ai* 情愛) as the Chinese characters can be interpreted in another context. No, to enlighten sentient beings is to empty yourself of love. You must see love as empty. That is to be a Bodhisattva.

Therefore, the verse says, *His mind is thus, thus unmoving, a superior one at peace.* "Thus, thus, unmoving" means there is no dharma that is not thus. All dharmas are thusness-Dharma and all afflictions and troubles have disappeared. To be unmoved is to have the power of samadhi. Doesn't the *Lotus Sutra* say, "His mind is at peace?" To be "at peace" this way is to be very happy and to possess great tranquility.

With total understanding of the ever-shining, he is host and master. You should have the total understanding of the ever-shining prajna wisdom. If you don't understand, then you do not shine; if you are not shining, then you don't understand. Therefore, you should understand and then understand even more, shine and shine even more. You should shine brightly in your total comprehension and totally comprehend in your shining brightness – that is understanding. You should be very clear.

What is being very clear? Being very clear is not being muddled and stupid. If you understand that to do a certain thing is wrong and you still go ahead and do it, that is piling stupidity on top of stupidity. You are doubly stupid. That is because you are not equal to being host. Being "host and master" is being able to be in control.

"I am master and I am host," someone says. "I tell everyone else to do anything I think they should be doing. I am not controlled by other people, but I myself control others. I won't do anything, so I just tell people to help me do my work, but I won't help them do theirs." No, being host and master is not like that. To be host and master is to be free of confusion and never to do anything confused.

To be in control at all times is to have genuine wisdom. You are without prejudice, and you don't act on the basis of deviant knowledge and views. You don't take drugs or do anything improper or disruptive. If you act improperly, then you get a chance to take a look at stupidity.

Six types of psychic powers are an ordinary matter. If you can be in control, you will naturally have the six psychic powers. They are:

1) the psychic power of the heavenly eye;
2) the psychic power of the heavenly ear;
3) psychic power with regard to past lives;
4) psychic power with regard to the minds of others;
5) the spiritually based psychic powers;
6) the psychic power of the extinction of outflows.

If you do not have the six types of psychic power, it is because you are not in control, because you are influenced by all the external circumstances you find yourself in. You are influenced by people and have no influence yourself to affect the situations that confront you. When you are able to turn situations around, then no matter what comes you will be unmoved. Don't be bold and say that you already know how, because to be unmoved means that even in a dream you are not affected by states of consciousness. That is to be host and master. If you are not affected by internal or external states, and if you have real wisdom and the six psychic powers, then you have a very ordinary talent working for you – nothing spectacular, just something very ordinary.

And even less can the winds and rains of the eight directions cause alarm. "The winds and rains of the eight directions" refers to the last two lines of a famous poem by *Su Dong Po* (1037-1101):

> *I bow to the god among gods;*
> *His hair-light illuminates the world.*
> *Unmoved when the eight winds blow,*
> *Upright I sit in a purple-gold lotus.*

Su Dong Po sent the poem to the Great Master *Fo-yin* (1011-1086), and the master's reply was two words: "Fart, fart." As soon as Su Dong Po saw Great Master Fo-yin's criticism, he couldn't get it out of his mind, and he rushed across the Yangtze – he lived on the south side of the river and Great Master Fo-yin lived on the north side – to find the master and scold him. He wanted to tell the master that he had written an enlightened poem, so how could the master possibly have replied, "Fart, fart?"

In fact, when Great Master Fo-yin criticized him, not only did Su Dong Po fart, he blazed forth and wanted to scorch Fo-yin to death. So he rushed across the river and burst into the master's quarters without ceremony and shouted, "How could you possibly scold someone and slander him that way by writing 'fart, fart'?"

Fo-yin replied, "Who was I slandering? You said that you were unmoved by the winds of the eight directions, but just by letting two small farts I've blown you all the way across the Yangtze. And you still say that the winds of the eight directions don't move you? You don't have to talk about eight winds; just my two farts bounced you all the way up here."

Then Su Dong Po thought, "That's right, I said that I'm unmoved by the eight winds, but two words have been enough to make me burn with anger." Realizing that he still didn't have what it takes, he bowed to the master and sought repentance.

What are the winds of the eight directions?

1) Praise. For example: "Upasaka[8], you are really a good person, you really understand the Buddhadharma, and your wisdom really shines. Furthermore, your genius is unlimited and your eloquence unobstructed."

2) Ridicule. For instance: "It's the scientific age now, and you are studying Buddhism. Why do you study that old superstitious rubbish?" Really ridiculous ridicule, and yet you think, "They're

---

[8.] Sanskrit term for a Buddhist layman.

right. How can I study Buddhism now in the scientific age? Cause and effect, no me and no you – how can such metaphysical theories be worth anything in the age of science? I am I, and people are people." You become confused and are moved by the blowing of the wind.

3) Suffering. The wind of suffering makes you suffer. To be unmoved while ceaselessly performing ascetic practices is an example of being unmoved by the wind of suffering.

4) Happiness. To eat well, to wear good clothes, to have a good place to live, and to be especially happy all day long, thinking, "This certainly is good," is to be moved by this wind.

5) Benefit. You think, "All I do is go to a lot of trouble cultivating. I don't even have any false thoughts. Consequently, people come to me and make an offering of a million dollars to build a temple, and they are very, very happy." That is to be moved by the wind of benefit.

6) Destruction. Perhaps the wind of benefit blew yesterday, but tomorrow people may come and ruin everything. They'll tell people, "That monk is no good. Don't believe in him; he will do anything. Believe in me instead."

7) Gain.

8) Loss.

Those are the eight winds. The verse says, "And even less can the winds and rains of the eight directions cause alarm." It means that the eight winds blow, but I don't move.

He rolls it up and secretly hides it away. When you close this sutra, you should store it in a good place, not a place that indicates your lack of respect. You should respect it.

And lets it go to fill the entire world. When you open it, the wisdom of prajna fills the sixfold union – that is, north, south, east, west, above, and below, which together represent the world. This prajna dharma-door is very wonderful.

Prajna and Emptiness

Sutra:

When Avalokiteshvara Bodhisattva was practicing the profound prajna paramita.

Verse:

> *Practice the Way, cultivate yourself,*
> *   and do not search outside.*
> *The prajna of your own nature*
> *   is the deep and secret cause.*
> *White billows soar to the heavens,*
> *   the black waves cease;*
> *Nirvana, the other shore,*
> *   effortlessly is climbed.*
> *Time and again, time and again,*
> *   don't miss the chance;*
> *Care for it, be diligent,*
> *   take hold of the divine innocence.*
> *Unclear mirage:*
> *   thus the news arrives;*
> *Now it's there, now it's not –*
> *   see what is originally esteemed.*

Commentary:

The word **practicing** in the sutra is simply what we understand as cultivation. As to **profound** it is the opposite of superficial. **Prajna** means wisdom, and **paramita** means to reach the other shore. The text says that Bodhisattva Avalokiteshvara cultivates profound, not superficial, prajna.

What is profound and what is superficial? Profound prajna is wonderful wisdom. Superficial prajna is limited to an understanding of the Four Truths and the Twelve Links of Conditioned Causation (*pratityasamutpada*) as studied in the Hinayana, the Small Vehicle. But only the wonderful wisdom of profound prajna can cause you to actually reach the other shore. Who is it who can arrive at the other shore? Avalokiteshvara Bodhisattva. When Shakyamuni Buddha spoke this sutra, he took special note of the great Bodhisattva Avalokiteshvara, who practices profound prajna and who has already reached the other shore. Thus the sutra says, **when Avalokiteshvara Bodhisattva was practicing the profound prajna paramita**. Those of the two vehicles, Arhats and Condition-Enlightened Ones, are unaware of profound prajna and cultivate only a superficial prajna, which is concerned with the analysis of emptiness. In their contemplations they make a very fine analysis of all form-dharmas and mind-dharmas.

What are form-dharmas and mind-dharmas? Form-dharmas are perceptible, while mind-dharmas are not. To make the distinction even clearer, everything that has perceptible characteristics and is conditioned is said to possess form. Since mind-dharmas are not perceptible objects, they can only be recognized as kinds of awareness. The fact that an awareness lacks any perceptible characteristics indicates that it is a mind-dharma, while what has perceptible characteristics but lacks awareness is called a form-dharma. Form-dharmas make up the first of the five skandhas, while feeling, cognition, formation, and consciousness, the remaining four skandhas, are all mind-dharmas, since they lack perceptible characteristics.

Therefore, **when Avalokiteshvara Bodhisattva was practicing the profound prajna paramita, he illuminated the five skandhas and saw that they are all empty.**

To talk about prajna is to talk about emptiness. Fundamentally there are many kinds of emptiness, but now for simplicity's sake, I will explain five basic kinds:

1) Insensate emptiness. This kind of emptiness lacks any knowing consciousness; it has no awareness. This emptiness, the ordinary emptiness known to most people, is called insensate emptiness because it consists merely of the emptiness we can see with our eyes, and it lacks its own awareness. It is the false, insensate emptiness people see in places where there is nothing at all. That lack of anything in a place is not the true emptiness.

2) The emptiness of annihilation. This is emptiness as it has been understood by those of certain external paths, none of whom understand the principle of true emptiness. They say that when people die they cease to exist, that is, they are annihilated. And so their version of emptiness is called the emptiness of annihilation.

3) The emptiness of analyzed dharmas. This emptiness is a contemplation cultivated by those of the Small Vehicle. They analyze form as form, mind as mind, and sort them into their constituent dharmas without realizing that they are all empty. They only go so far as to say that because a perceptible characteristic can be analyzed as one of various form-dharmas, that because feeling, cognition, formation, and consciousness can be analyzed in terms of various mind-dharmas, they are empty. As a consequence, those of the two vehicles are not certified as ones who have accomplished the wonderful meaning of true emptiness. They stop at the transformation city[9]. They stand there, at that empty and false place,

---

9. The enlightenment of those of the two vehicles (Arhats and Pratyekabuddhas) is compared to a city conjured up by magic that has no real existence. The source of the well-known image is the *Dharma Flower Sutra* (*Suddharmapundarika-sutra*). A reference to the same analogy is found further on in the verse commentary: *Partial truth with residue is just a conjured city.*

cultivating the contemplation of the emptiness of analyzed dharmas. That is what is called superficial prajna, not profound prajna.

Cultivators of superficial prajna can end the birth and death of their delimited segment (Sanskrit *pariccheda*; Chinese *fen duan* 分段 literally "share-section"), but they are unable to transcend the birth and death of the fluctuations (Sanskrit *parinama*; Chinese *bian yi* 變易). What is meant by these two kinds of birth and death? The first refers to the body, and the second to thoughts. Everyone has a body; you have yours, I have mine, everyone has his own "share". The body is a share and one lifetime from birth to death is called a section. It could also be said that everyone has his own form-section: you are five feet tall, he is five foot six inches, and that person is six feet tall. Each person has his own section, so this is the birth and death of one's "share-section" or delimited segment.

The Holy Ones of the fourth stage of Arhatship have ended the birth and death of their delimited segments, but they have not yet ended the birth and death of fluctuations. "Fluctuations" refers to the transformations which are the source of the birth and death of the delimited segment, because the birth and death of fluctuations refers to nothing more than all the various false thoughts. The false thoughts flow along: one thought ceases to exist and the next thought is born; then that thought ceases to exist and a third is born, and so forth. That kind of successive production and extinction is also a kind of birth and death. At the fourth stage of Arhatship, false thinking has not been extinguished entirely. The stage of the Bodhisattva of the Mahayana, the Great Vehicle, must be reached in order to put an end to the birth and death of fluctuations. Then there are no more false thoughts.

The birth and death of fluctuations is at the root of our birth and death. Why is it that we are born and then die? Only because we have false thoughts. And where do the false thoughts come from? From ignorance. It is because there is ignorance that all false thoughts are produced.

4) Bodily dharma emptiness. The fourth kind of emptiness is cultivated by the Condition-Enlightened Ones, the Pratyeka-buddhas, who have the bodily experience of the emptiness of dharmas.

5) True emptiness. Bodhisattvas cultivate the contemplation of the emptiness of wonderful existence. **When Avalokiteshvara Bodhisattva was practicing the profound prajna paramita**, he was cultivating the contemplation of the emptiness of wonderful existence. When he **illuminated the five skandhas and saw that they are all empty**, he was cultivating at the level reached by profound prajna with the ability obtained from profound prajna.

Practice the Way, cultivate yourself, and do not search outside. If you wish to cultivate the Way, don't look outside yourself, for outside there is nothing to be sought. You should search within your own nature.

The prajna of your own nature is the deep and secret cause means that deep within your own nature lies the secret seed.

White billows soar to the heavens, the black waves cease. When one cultivates the Way, the white billows, which are like waves of rolling water, are wisdom, and the black waves are affliction. When affliction has ceased, your wisdom soars on high. Thus the profound prajna paramita which the Bodhisattva practices is both high and deep. It is deep because when you are in that high place you look down and don't see anything at all.

Nirvana, the other shore, effortlessly is climbed. With wisdom you can very naturally reach the other shore of Nirvana; very, very easily, very, very naturally you get to the other shore, without any need to expend any effort at all.

Time and again, time and again, don't miss the chance. The time when we cultivate the Way is the most precious, so don't let it go by emptily. "Time and again, time and again." Don't let the time in which we should cultivate prajna paramita go by emptily; don't let it go by!

Care for it, be diligent, take hold of the divine innocence. When you are filled with energy and alive with spirit, you should not forget to pay attention. You should not let that time go by, because that is the time to cultivate and to attain true prajna – the doctrine of the divine innocence[10].

Unclear mirage; thus the news arrives. The events are likened to an unclear mirage. You wish to see them, yet you look at them and don't see them. You listen, yet you don't hear anything. At the time when your seeing is like an unclear mirage, you get a little news.

Now it's there, now it's not – see what is originally esteemed. You look and say what you see is real, but it doesn't seem to have any perceptible characteristic. Then you say it doesn't have any perceptible characteristic, yet it seems like you are seeing something. What you see is what is originally esteemed – your own nature.

---

[10]. *tian zhen* 天真, the natural spontaneity that sage and child alike possess.

The Conditioned Body

Sutra:

He illuminated the five skandhas and saw that they are all empty.

Verse:

> *The three lights shine everywhere,*
> *   permeating the three forces.*
> *The one returns to the place of union,*
> *   yet the one comes forth again.*
> *See that form is emptiness and that feeling*
> *   is the same way;*
> *False thoughts are the shifting currents,*
> *   while formation is the arranger of karma;*
> *With consciousness, which understands differences,*
> *   the five shadows are completed.*
> *Mirror-flowers and water-moon,*
> *   beyond defiling dust:*
> *Emptiness not empty – the great function of clarity;*
> *Vision is yet not a view – happiness indeed!*

Commentary:

The three lights shine everywhere, permeating the three forces. "The three lights" are the sun, the moon, and the stars, which illuminate everything in the universe and thoroughly penetrate "the three forces" of heaven, earth, and humanity. The three lights are also the lights of wisdom: the light of the prajna of language, the light of the prajna of contemplative illumination, and the light of the prajna of the characteristic of actuality[11]. The light of true prajna of the characteristic of actuality is the very deep prajna-light by which **Avalokiteshvara Bodhisattva illuminated the five skandhas and saw that they are all empty**. With the three kinds of light he illuminates every place in the heavens and on earth, and the lights permeate the three motive forces.

The one returns to the place of union, yet the one comes forth again. "The one" refers to one's own nature. The "place of union" is where one's own nature dwells. Basically it is this: "Ten thousand dharmas return to one; one returns to unity." So says the verse about Shen Guang[12]:

> *Ten thousand dharmas return to one,*
> *The one returns to unity[13].*
> *Shen-kuang didn't understand,*
> *And ran after Bodhidharma; before*
> *Him by Bear Ear Mountain knelt*
> *Nine years seeking Dharma*
> *To escape King Yama.*

The "one" that the ten thousand dharmas return to is the mind or nature of each individual. The "one returning to unity" is the uniting with the Buddhanature.

After uniting with the Buddhanature, "the one comes forth again"; this is the giving birth to the wonderful functioning of the

---

[11.] The three are also said to be the symbolic red, white, and purple lights.

[12.] Also known as *Hui Guo*, was the second Patriarch of the Chan School of Buddhism in China.

[13.] According to a textual variant, the second line of the verse reads, "To what does the one return?"

one, which is the Buddhahood you realize. The one that comes forth again is just you, this Buddha.

See that form is emptiness and feeling is the same way. You can see form, yet it is fundamentally empty. The sutra says that **form itself is emptiness**; what does this mean? We common people are attached to form, to a general form-body in which the many kinds of form-dharmas are united. This is what we call our physical body. "How can we say that the form-body is empty?" someone says. "It's really here! It wears clothes, eats, sleeps, so how can it be empty?" When you understand how form can exist, you can be empty.

I spoke earlier about the emptiness of analyzed dharmas. The body is analyzed as the summation of the characteristics of form which are united together. This is the way it is. Earth, water, fire, and wind, the four great elements (*mahabhuta*), are the differentiated characteristics of form. The form-body comes into being when earth, water, fire, and wind unite. The skin, flesh, muscles, and bones of our bodies are the great element earth. The saliva, urine, excrement, water, and sweat are the great element water. The heat of our bodies is the great element fire; and the circulation of the breath is the great element wind. The four great elements unite to become a body, and when they separate, the body is destroyed. Each of the four elements returns to its original position, which is emptiness.

Most people are attached to the body as "me". That's wrong; the body is not "me". "Then what is 'me'?" you ask. You can control your body and have the perceptions of seeing, hearing, smelling, tasting, touching, and knowing. It is the perception-nature which is me. "So then what is the body?" One can only say, "This body is mine," not "This body is me." The body is like a house; you live in a house, but you do not say, "This house is me." If you were to say that, everyone would laugh their teeth right out of their mouths. But when you refer to your body as "me", most people don't laugh, because they also live with the same supposition. But it is just the same as supposing that your house is you. Because you live in a body-house, you say it is you. In the body there are seeing, smelling, hearing, tasting, feeling, and knowing. But are those the Buddhanature? It is the Buddhanature which is you.

The body comes into being merely through the gathering together of conditioned causes. If the conditioned causes set themselves up in a different manner, then the form-body disperses. That is the reason one cannot say, "My body is me." One can only say, "It is mine. This is my body, and I can disown it or exchange it for another." You have that kind of authority, but you yourself don't know it yet. Because you live in the house, you don't know about the events which go on outside. You still suppose, "This house is me." Don't perceive the house as being you.

If we take a look into form and analyze it, form itself is empty – it doesn't exist. Therefore, it follows that emptiness can be changed into form-dharma. How does the change take place? Earth, water, fire, and wind merge to become a body. It has been said that God created people. His work of creation was just a matter of putting earth, fire, water, and wind together. If we use earth, fire, water, and wind, we can also create a person, or a lot of people. Anybody could do it. A few materials are used, and a person is created. When the conditioned causes come together, a person comes into being; when the conditioned causes disperse, the person ceases to exist.

If you understand that **form itself is emptiness**, then you shouldn't perceive the body as "me". It is only a possession; it just belongs to "me". But here especially you should not be attached. If you take the attitude that "the body is what I have," then you will want to help it a lot, and you will "make your mind your body's slave."[14] Here "mind" means your awakened mind, which can understand that your body is a form-dharma and thereby unreal.

[14.] The quotation is from Tao Yuan Ming's celebrated poem "Returning Home". In the poem the poet talks about returning from an official position which he felt compromised his principles.

Therefore, don't be attached to it. Destroy the form skandha, and the form skandha will be empty.

"See that form is emptiness and feeling is the same way." Feeling, the second of the five skandhas is like form; it's empty.

False thoughts are the shifting currents; this refers to the cognition-skandha. *While formation is the arranger of karma*; this is the formation-skandha. The karma created from formation is arranged together in an orderly fashion.

With consciousness which understands differences: the consciousness-skandha is fine discrimination and understanding of differences. *The five shadows are completed.* Form, feeling, cognition, formation, and consciousness are the five skandhas, which are often represented in Chinese by the character *yin* 陰, which literally means shadow.

Mirror-flowers and water-moon, beyond defiling dust. The five skandhas – form, feeling, thought, formation, and conscious-ness – are like flowers reflected in a mirror, or like the image of the moon on the surface of the water. No dust at all defiles them, for the five skandhas are all empty.

Emptiness not empty – the great function of clarity. When you don't understand clearly that the five skandhas are all empty, there is affliction, false thinking, and trouble. It is just within clarity about the five skandhas that you turn your consciousness around to realize wisdom. Doing just that is the especially great and wonderful functioning which you then understand.

Vision is yet not a view – happiness indeed! True emptiness produces wonderful existence. The production of wonderful existence has a great use. "Vision is yet not a view" means that then your seeing is the same as not seeing. When you are unaffected by this kind of experience, you attain genuine happiness. Therefore, the verse says, "Happiness indeed!"

The Kinds of Suffering

Sutra:

And he crossed beyond all suffering and difficulty.

Commentary:

All refers to everything which is suffering and difficulty. **Suffering** by itself is already unpleasant to endure; add **difficulty** to suffering and the suffering is even greater. **Crossed beyond** indicates deliverance from suffering and the attainment of happiness; it means liberation. "Why then doesn't the sutra simply say 'liberated', instead of **crossed beyond all suffering and difficulty**?" you ask. Even if you illuminate the five skandhas and see that they are all empty as Bodhisattva Avalokiteshvara did, you still must cultivate. Only then can you cross beyond all suffering and difficulty. To illuminate emptiness and see it is merely to know emptiness; you must still practice. Although you have quickly awakened to the principle, there is still the gradual work of cultivation.

If you know about emptiness but don't cultivate, then emptiness is of no use. If you understand that the principle itself is empty, you should cultivate and cross beyond suffering and difficulty. If you want to cultivate, you yourself must actually do it. It's not just talk-Zen: "Hey! I've become enlightened. I've attained *anuttarasam-yaksambodhi*, the Utmost Right and Perfect Enlightenment." Enlightened? How did you become enlightened? How did you do it? How was your *anuttarasamyaksambodhi* certified? It's easy to say, but hard to do! Just saying it is a dharma, but by doing it you arrive. If you say it, you must be able to do it. If you know about emptiness, then you should cultivate. Understand true emptiness, then cultivate wonderful existence.

The suffering and difficulty which is crossed beyond is not limited to just one kind of suffering. All kinds are included: the three kinds of suffering, the eight kinds, and all the infinite kinds. The three kinds of suffering are: the suffering of suffering itself; the suffering of decay; the suffering of the activity of the five skandhas. The three sufferings are also called the three kinds of feeling: the feeling of suffering, the feeling of happiness, and the feeling of neither happiness nor suffering. Therefore, the suffering of suffering itself is the feeling of suffering, and the suffering of decay is the feeling of happiness. You shouldn't try to refute this by thinking that happiness is not caught up in suffering, because happiness can go bad. Happiness going bad is the suffering of decay. The suffering of the activity of the five skandhas refers to feelings which are neither happy nor unhappy. That one doesn't hold any interest either.

The first four of the eight kinds of suffering are: the suffering of birth; the suffering of old age; the suffering of sickness; the suffering of death. Who isn't born? At the moment of birth, you suffer. And who can prevent old age? Yet one might say, "A child died before it had a chance to grow old; since it did not get old, it basically didn't have any awareness." However, even though it wasn't old, it still suffered sickness and death, and one could also say that it suffered growing old, for the day it died it was old. If it had not become old, how could it have died? Because it died, one can also say the child changed to become old and endured the suffering of old age, even though its life did not bear fruit.

Who dares to say that sickness is not suffering? Sickness is especially bitter suffering. Even when one who has become enlightened gets sick, he still suffers in the same way. For example, Shakyamuni Buddha suffered from the retribution of the metal spear and the retribution of the horse-feed. Why did he have to undergo those retributions? When Shakyamuni Buddha was a child on the causal ground of a former life, he lived in a place where the populace was starving. One day the starving people pulled a great fish up from the sea to the shore. Before they had a chance to eat it, the child who was to be Shakyamuni Buddha picked up a big stick, approached the fish, and hit it on the head several times. Even after he realized Buddhahood, Shakyamuni Buddha's head often hurt as if it were being pricked with a spear. That was the retribution of the metal spear.

On the causal ground of a former life, Shakyamuni Buddha spoke wrongly to a cultivator of the Way. He said to the cultivator, "Your cultivation is still lacking in sufficient ascetic practices. If you were really cultivating, you would be eating horse-feed." After Shakyamuni Buddha attained Buddhahood, he was invited to a certain country to dwell in peaceful retreat for the summer, but the king didn't make offerings to him and only gave him and his bhikshus, the Buddhist monks who were his disciples, horse-feed to eat. This was the horse-feed retribution. The karma which you create on the causal ground must be undergone as retribution on the ground which is its fruition.

After the suffering of birth, old age, and sickness comes the suffering of death. Death: nobody welcomes it. Why? Probably because it is suffering.

The second four of the eight kinds of suffering are: the suffering of being apart from those you love; the suffering of being together with those you despise; the suffering of not obtaining what you seek; the suffering of the flourishing of the five skandhas.

Because there are all those kinds, the sutra says **all suffering**. By cultivating, it is possible to avoid the three kinds of suffering, the eight kinds of suffering, and all the infinite kinds of suffering. That is what the sutra means by **crossed beyond all suffering and difficulty**. I have written a verse about it:

Verse:

Across the sea of suffering,
   one leaves the revolving wheel.
The rains disperse, the heavens clears;
   just then the moon is fully bright.
The qian source is the Way-substance,
   among people the sage.
His undecaying golden body
   is rare in the world.
Cast off life;
   what need of thousand-year drugs?
Attain extinction;
   why wait ten thousand kalpas?
Five dwellings ended,
   the two deaths disappear forever.
Roam at will from East to West,
   throughout the dharma realm.

Commentary:

Across the sea of suffering, one leaves the revolving wheel. "The sea of suffering" is just **all suffering and difficulty**. If you wish to cross beyond all suffering and difficulty, you must first be released from the revolving wheel of the six paths of rebirth: gods, asuras, people, animals, hungry ghosts, and hell-dwellers.

The rains disperse, the heavens clear; just then the moon is fully bright. The time of release from the paths of rebirth is likened to the time when the rain stops, the heavens clear, and the full moon is filling the sky with its radiance. The line represents the emptiness of all five skandhas:

The bright moon stands out upon the sky;
There are no clouds for ten thousand miles.

That is what you experience as soon as you give birth to genuine wisdom and are enlightened to all. Then you have **crossed beyond all suffering and difficulty**.

The qian source is the Way-substance, among people the sage. When you have been certified as having reached the first stage of Arhatship, it can be said that your body is pure *yang*. In the *I Ching* (*The Book of Changes*), *qian* 乾, the first hexagram, represents pure *yang* substance.

His undecaying golden body is rare in the world. When you have been certified as having reached the first stage, that is, when you have cut off the eighty-eight categories of deluded views, your body is flawless gold, very, very rare in the world.

Cast off life; what need of thousand-year drugs? Emperor Shi of the Qin Dynasty (221-207 B.C.) sought the Taoist elixir of immortality, and even sent an expedition to the Isles of the Peng Lai Immortals. Yet you do not need to search for elixirs of immortality. Just cross beyond all suffering and difficulty, and then if you wish to live, you can live, and if you wish to die, you can die. Just as with Bodhidharma, birth and death will be your own, and Yama, the lord of death, won't be able to have anything to do with you.

Attain extinction; why wait ten thousand kalpas? Extinction is the third of the Four Truths of suffering, accumulating, extinction, and the Way. If you can have your extinction certified, you can attain nirvana. Having realized the Way, you don't need ten thousand kalpas but can quickly attain the nirvana without residue (*anupadisesanirvana*).

Five dwellings ended, the two deaths disappear forever. When you have really crossed beyond all suffering and difficulty, have left the revolving wheel, and have obtained an indestructible vajra body, "the two deaths disappear forever." "Two deaths," you say. "Does that mean that you have to die twice?" No, it refers to the two kinds of birth and death: the birth and death of the delimited segment of the body, and the birth and death of the fluctuations of thoughts. The birth and death of the delimited segment is ended by those who have been certified as having attained Arhatship. To end the birth and death of the fluctuations, Bodhisattvahood must first be attained. Avalokiteshvara has attained Bodhisattvahood, and so the birth and death of the fluctuations is no more. Both deaths have disappeared.

The "five dwellings" refer to the five dwellings in affliction, which are,

1) dwelling in views, which originally was called dwelling in the love of views;
2) dwelling in the love of desire;
3) dwelling in the love of form;
4) dwelling in the love of the formless;
5) dwelling in the love of ignorance.

Those five ways of abiding in love cause attachments which change into five kinds of affliction. Avalokiteshvara makes the five afflictions cease, and from that follows the last line of the verse, to which you should pay a little attention:

Roam at will from East to West, throughout the dharma realm. "Roam" indicates ease, freedom, and being very, very happy. In what way? You can travel wherever you wish. "At will from East to West": you can go to the Western Paradise any time you want, or you can travel to the East, to the crystal world of Akshobhya Buddha. There's even less problem about going to this suffering Saha world right here. You have avoided the troublesome preparation of applying at a consulate for a visa. You just wish to go and then go.

Not just to the east and west, but to the north and south, up and down, to the ten directions all around; the whole dharma realm is included. Wherever you go you are welcome. It's not that you want to travel to someplace, but find yourself unwelcome. Wherever you want to go you can go, and you are never unwelcome. To roam at will from East to West throughout the dharma realm is to be genuinely happy, genuinely carefree, truly at ease, truly free and equal; it is the truly real and equal nature of the dharma realm. When the five dwellings have been ended and when the two deaths disappear forever, this kind of freedom is attained.

Shariputra

Sutra:

Shariputra.

Verse:

> *Shariputra is the solid and durable proof;*
> *The name means "pelican" –*
> * the demeanor of his mother.*
> *With precepts and samadhi complete and bright,*
> * the pearl-light appears;*
> *Practice and understanding interact,*
> * and his body is transparent.*
> *How does there come to be great wisdom?*
> * Because the stupid make their mark.*
> *Already in his mother's womb*
> * a fine eloquence had been born;*
> *This real wisdom is complete within all people;*
> *Grasp it at Jewelled Wood Peak at Cao Creek.*

Commentary:

In speaking the *Heart of Prajna Paramita Sutra*, the Buddha addressed his disciple, **Shariputra**, foremost in wisdom among the Buddha's disciples. *Shariputra is the solid and durable proof.* The name Shariputra means solid and durable; that is, the wisdom of Shariputra is solid and durable.

The name means "pelican" – the demeanor of his mother. The *shari* is a large sea bird of the pelican genus. It flies high and has telescopic vision. When the fish swim near the surface of the sea, the bird shoots down from high in the sky as fast as a rocket, scoops up the fish, and eats them. It is able to do it because it can see very clearly.

In India children were named according to the father's name, the mother's name, or both the father's and mother's names. Shariputra received his name from his mother's line. His mother was called *Shari* because of the nature of her demeanor. *Putra* means son, so the son of *Shari* was called Shariputra.

With precepts and samadhi complete and bright, the pearl light appears. In previous lives, life after life, Shariputra had cultivated precepts, samadhi, and wisdom to full brightness and perfection, and at that point the pearl-light appears.[15]

Practice and understanding interact, and his body is transparent. He both studied the teachings and cultivated them, so his wisdom was especially great, and his body was transparent like glass.

How does there come to be great wisdom? Because the stupid make their mark. What is great wisdom? Most stupid people have their own special style of behavior, but Shariputra was not like them. Stupid people do things in an upside-down way: they speak clearly about what they will do, but when they do it, they do it poorly. That's stupidity. The great wisdom of Shariputra was beyond confusion. Because he knew clearly, he never purposely allowed wrong to be done, and he was never upside down.

[15.] The pearl refers to the *sharira* (or relic) said to be a physical manifestation of the above-mentioned perfections. The relics of enlightened beings resemble effulgent pearls.

Already in his mother's womb a fine eloquence had been born. You all remember that Shariputra's mother and her brother often debated and that his mother could never outwit her brother. But when she was pregnant with Shariputra, she was always able to defeat her brother in debate. Since he couldn't out-talk his sister, he realized that she was about to give birth to an outstanding child, and he went off to study the doctrines of external paths so that he would not lose face before his nephew. But when he returned, Shariputra had already left home to follow Shakyamuni Buddha.[16]

This real wisdom is complete within all people. It is not only the venerable Shariputra who has great wisdom; everyone has this genuine wisdom. But not everyone uses it; most people forget about it. But everyone has it and has the capability of using it.

Grasp it at Jewelled Wood Peak at Cao Creek. Where is this real wisdom? It's at Cao Creek, and Cao Creek is at Nan-hua Monastery in Ma-pa Township in Kuangtong Province, China. The

---

[16.] The uncle, realizing that the child would be of uncommon intelligence and not wanting to lose face, went away from home. He travelled all over India and diligently studied all the extant works on logic, philosophy, and religion. Seventeen years later he returned home, only to find that his nephew had left the home-life to follow the Buddha. Angered that he had lost the brilliant child, he went to retrieve him. When he arrived at the place where the Buddha was dwelling, he challenged the Buddha to a debate on the following terms: if he were to win, then the Buddha would allow Shariputra to leave and become the uncle's disciple. If he were to lose, the Buddha could have his head.

The Buddha agreed and asked him to state his basic premise. The uncle replied that it was the non-acceptance of all dharmas, thinking that by the use of such a premise no matter what the Buddha said in debate he would not have to accept it. However, the Buddha then asked, "Do you accept that view or not?" The uncle then realized that if he did, it would be in violation of his own premise, and that if he didn't, the premise would no longer hold either.

Then, fearing the loss of his head, the uncle impulsively ran away. Yet after running a considerable distance, he stopped to consider his action and returned to offer his head to the Buddha. The Buddha refused his head but accepted him as a disciple. He became one of the ten great disciples of the Buddha and was known by the name Mahakausthila.

Nan-hua Monastery of Jewelled Wood Mountain is Cao Creek, the Bodhimanda of the Sixth Patriarch.

"Oh," you think, "that's so far! How could I possibly go there to grasp it? Not only have the Communists sealed the borders, but even if they would let me in, it is too far and I do not have the means to get there."

That's good, for it isn't necessary to go. Each one of you has the Jewelled Wood Peak at Cao Creek, and it is unnecessary to travel far to seek it. The wisdom is within you. How do you meet it? Put down your upside-down mind; let go of your false-thinking mind. Earnestly work hard at your meditation. When you sit in meditation and look into Chan, just that is Jewelled Wood Peak at Cao Creek.

Form Does Not Differ From Emptiness

Sutra:

Form does not differ from emptiness; emptiness does not differ from form. Form itself is emptiness; emptiness itself is form.

Verse:

> *"Form does not differ from emptiness":*
> *"is" is like "is not".*
> *"Emptiness does not differ from form":*
> *the distinction is of substance and function.*
> *"Form itself is emptiness":*
> *its true source is fathomed.*
> *"Emptiness itself is form":*
> *the false flow has dried up.*
> *Mountains, rivers, and the great earth*
> *are only manifestations of consciousness.*
> *"Dream, illusion, bubble, shadow" – so it is!*
> *Be careful not to seek outside;*
> *maintain the Middle Way.*
> *To cast down stained threads of cause*
> *is to come toward the Thus.*

Commentary:

What is **form**? That which has a perceptible characteristic is form. What is **emptiness**? That which is without characteristics is emptiness. Then why does the text say, **form does not differ from emptiness; emptiness does not differ from form; form itself is emptiness** and **emptiness itself is form**? The sutra declares the ultimate meaning which penetrates clearly to the most fundamental principle.

The mountains, the rivers, the great earth, and all the chambers, corridors, rooms, and dwellings are **form**. What is form? Form is within emptiness. Where then is emptiness? Emptiness is within form. **Form** and **emptiness** are therefore said to be non-dual. **Form does not differ from emptiness** means that they do not have differing characteristics.

Emptiness does not differ from form also indicates that emptiness and form do not have different characteristics. They are one. Emptiness contains form, and form contains emptiness. On the surface, two are seen, yet the actuality is one.

To discuss form, let us consider the example of a table. Put it in a certain empty place, and it occupies the emptiness of that place so that the emptiness no longer exists. Take the table away and the emptiness immediately reappears. The place is then empty. Before the table was taken away, did the emptiness exist? Yes, there was emptiness, but it was occupied by the form. The empty space certainly was not non-existent. Now, where there is emptiness, is there form? Just there lies the origin of form. That is the form which is emptiness. We have taken a look into form and analyzed it so that it has become empty.

What are they like? The body is characterized as a form-dharma, while the mind is categorized as emptiness. Mind-dharma is emptiness-dharma; the attainment of the principle of true emptiness is mind. Since the body is a form-dharma, from what does it come into existence? It is composed of earth, water, fire, and wind, the four great elements, which come together and become a form-body. Further, there is a place to which each of the four great elements returns. When a person dies, the water returns to the great element water, the earth returns to the great element earth, the fire returns to the great element fire, and the wind returns to the great element wind. Each has a place it returns to, so that the form no longer exists. Thus the sutra says that **form itself is emptiness** and that **form does not differ from emptiness**. Although there is the characteristic of form now, in the future it will be emptied. Thus the verse says, *"Form does not differ from emptiness;" "is" is like "is not"*. Although something "is", the "is" is the same as "is not".

"Emptiness does not differ from form": the distinction is of substance and function. Emptiness and form are not different, yet they may be considered in terms of substance and function. Emptiness refers to empty substance, while form is the function of emptiness. Although substance and function appear to be distinct, they are fundamentally one.

"Form itself is emptiness": its true source is fathomed. When you actually know that **form itself is emptiness**, its true source is fathomed. Your true source is reached and you thoroughly understand.

"Emptiness itself is form": the false flow has dried up. When you actually understand that **emptiness itself is form**, there is no false thinking: the "false flow" ceases.

Form does not differ from emptiness; emptiness does not differ from form. It can be said that this experience is a particular attainment in your cultivation of the Way. It might also be said that the form referred to is all the varieties of "beautiful form," a Chinese figure of speech for sexual matters. **Form does not differ from emptiness**. The kind of pleasure obtained from real experiences of attainment from cultivating the Way may seem the same as the happiness derived from "form-dharmas." Therefore, **form does not differ from emptiness**, and **emptiness does not differ from form**. Here you have obtained bliss from your cultivation which surpasses that of male-female relations more than a hundred trillion-fold.

Therefore, if in form you are able to understand the principle of emptiness and not get attached, neither grasping nor rejecting nor receiving, that is emptiness. **Emptiness does not differ from form**, for **emptiness itself is form**. In emptiness you experience genuine happiness, and "the false flow has dried up." At that time your false thinking has ceased to exist as well. Why? You have obtained a happiness which is even greater than that derived from form. You have let go of the false-thinking mind.

Mountains, rivers, and the great earth are only manifestations of consciousness. Mountains, rivers, and the great earth are all form-dharmas which appear because of the consciousness in our minds which makes distinctions. If we can transform the consciousness which makes distinctions, then all the mountains and rivers and the great earth will not exist.

"Dream, illusion, bubble, shadow" – so it is![17] All is like a dream. Everyone knows about dreams because everyone has them, but if I ask you why you had a particular dream, your reply may seem to be correct, but it will not necessarily be accurate. You might say, "What I do during the day I dream about at night." Or perhaps you will say, "In the past I experienced something, and as a consequence I had a dream about it." However, you sometimes dream about things that you have no previous experience of. How do you explain that? You can't, and you can't say how you awoke from the dream either. This is to be murky and mixed up. As soon as you awake from a dream, you forget it. Think about that. You have a dream, and after less than ten hours have passed you have forgotten it entirely.

[17.] The quotation is from the final verse of the *Diamond Sutra*:

All conditioned dharmas
Are like dreams, illusions, bubbles, shadows,
Like dew drops and a lightning flash:
Contemplate them thus.

Now let's consider the contents of our past lives. You are thinking, "I don't believe there are past lives. If I had past lives, why don't I remember them?" Take the dream as a comparison. The day passes and the dream of the night before is forgotten. How much the less can we remember the events of our past lives!

If a person is dreaming about being rich and prominent and someone appears in the dream and says to the dreamer, "You are rich and a great official and you have many sons and daughters and a lot of property, but none of it is real; it is just a dream," the dreamer can't believe it is true, and he replies, "What? I have amassed great wealth, am a high official, have many sons and daughters and vast properties. How can I be dreaming?" Regardless of what happens, the dreamer doesn't believe that he is in a dream.

Upon waking, he realizes without being told that he was dreaming. "When I made so much money and was an official and had many sons and daughters and vast properties, it all was only a dream. It wasn't true." Without being told, he knows. Why? Because he has awakened from his dream.

You should know that now we too are dreaming. I am telling you right now that you are dreaming, but you can't believe it. Wait until you cultivate, cultivate to understanding, and, "Ah, everything I did before was all a dream." You have done no more than dreamed. Upon waking you will know, know from the ground up, "I was dreaming before; all that came before was a dream." This is what is meant by the word "dream" in the verse.

What is meant by "illusion?" For instance, a magician creates something from nothing; he can also make something turn into nothing. However, although such illusions of change are not fathomed by small children who see the magic as real, adults see through the deception of the magician's transformations. They recognize the illusion for what it is.

"Bubble" refers to bubbles of water, which burst after not very long. They are impermanent.

"Shadow" refers specifically to a person's shadow. Is a person's shadow real? You may say the shadow is unreal, but look at it: there it is, existent. If you say that it is real, try to grab it; you cannot. You look and there's a shadow; you try to gather it up with your hand but can't catch hold. So is it real or isn't it? Say it is unreal, yet it still exists; say it is real, yet it can't be gathered up.

Where does the shadow come from? It is found on the north side of your body. On the *yang* side, the sunny southern side, there is no shadow. On the *yin* side, the shadow follows you wherever you go. The shadow I am talking about in the verse is an analogy. Like a ghost, it follows you wherever you go. As soon as people who are afraid of ghosts see a dark shadow, their hearts respond with great fear. Their hearts go thump, thump, thump. "Ohh, a ghost has come!" It's a ghost, although, originally it was just a shadow.

When you are alive, the shadow is just a shadow, but when you die and don't have your body, the shadow becomes a ghost, and the side which does not have a shadow changes into a god. The god and the ghost, however, are not two; they are one. If you are full of *yang* energy, you move to the side where there is no shadow; if you are full of *yin* energy, you move to the shaded side. You move to the side where your strength is greater. If you have a lot of merit, you rise into the heavens. If the karma of your offenses is greater, you fall into the hells. Therefore, the verse says, "'Dream, illusion, bubble, shadow' – so it is!" That's just the way it is.

Be careful not to seek outside; maintain the Middle Way. You shouldn't seek outside yourself; it is all there within you.

To cast down stained threads of cause is to come toward the Thus. What are stained threads of cause? Thoughts of desire.

> *Greed in the mind is a stained thread of cause;*
> *Hatred in the mind is a stained thread of cause;*
> *Stupidity in the mind is a stained thread of cause;*
> *The taking of life is a stained thread of cause;*
> *Stealing is a stained thread of cause;*

Deviant desires are stained threads of cause;
False speech is a stained thread of cause;
Alcohol, drugs, and the like
  are stained threads of cause.

Cast down all the stained threads of cause, and join the family of the Thus Come One, the Tathagata. To have cast down the stained threads of cause is to have come close to the realization of Buddhahood, to have "come toward the Thus." One who has realized Buddhahood is called the Thus Come One. Not having realized Buddhahood, we are said to be "coming toward the Thus." Only when we have arrived can we become "thus." If we have not arrived, we are not "thus." Arrived where? Where the Buddha is. "Thus" is everything fully united with principle, with the noumenon. Not the smallest thing is wrong; everything is right. Just that is "to come toward the Thus."

Emptiness is true emptiness, and **form** is wonderful existence. True emptiness is not empty, because it is wonderful existence. Wonderful existence is not existence, because it is also true emptiness. From what place does emptiness appear? It appears where there is existence, from form-dharmas. Because form-dharmas also appear within emptiness, the sutra says, **form does not differ from emptiness; emptiness does not differ from form. Form itself is emptiness; emptiness itself is form**. That is to say, true emptiness is not empty, and wonderful existence is not existence. To understand in the midst of unknowing: that is to fathom the fundamental source of the Dharma; that is your genuine understanding of the Buddhadharma.

Take, for example, the dream I just discussed. If you don't understand dreams and the source of their coming and the pulse of their going – if you don't understand how you had the dream and how you awakened from the dream – then you don't know how you came to be born, either, or how you will die. To understand while not knowing: that is enlightenment. Therefore, the verse reads,

"'Form itself is emptiness: its true source is fathomed." In enlightenment you understand this truth.

"'Emptiness itself is form: the false flow dries up." False thinking is cut off, so that it no longer exists.

If you want to comprehend the doctrine of emptiness and existence, you should take a look at that very place where there is neither emptiness nor form. The Great Master Hui Neng, the Sixth Patriarch, said, "With no thoughts of good and no thoughts of evil, at just this moment what is the Superior One Hui-ming's original face?" "With no thoughts of good" is not being empty, and "with no thoughts of evil" is not having form. The place where there are neither thoughts of good nor thoughts of evil is where there is neither emptiness nor existence. You should come and look into it, and become enlightened where there is both emptiness and existence. Then you will be capable of understanding that **form does not differ from emptiness**, and **emptiness does not differ from form**.

In true emptiness is true form; in true form is true emptiness. It follows that the form-dharma is the original substance of emptiness, and the emptiness-dharma is the face of form. Therefore, I have said that in the form-dharma there is emptiness, and in the emptiness-dharma there is form.

For instance, a mountain is a form-dharma; if you level the mountain, then emptiness appears. Before the mountain was leveled, did that emptiness exist or didn't it? Yes, it did. "When there is emptiness, does form exist as well?" Form is there, too. So you can see that where there is emptiness, form can also exist. Emptiness and form are one.

Form and emptiness are analogous to ice and water. Why is there form? In emptiness occurs the transformation into ice. In emptiness a fine dust collects, congeals together, and becomes a form. When it disperses, there is emptiness. Therefore, emptiness is form, and form is emptiness. How does the transformation into form occur? When the weather is cold, the cold in the air changes water into ice. That is the way the transformation from emptiness to form occurs. How does form change into emptiness? The weather gets hot and melts the ice. "But," you say, "dust cannot melt." Remember, this is just an analogy and does not imply that dust is ice.

Because I was afraid that you wouldn't understand the principle, I lent you the analogy of ice and water. Don't seize upon it and suppose that dust and emptiness can be transformed into water and ice. Thinking that way is just piling another head on top of your head. Such attachments are fundamentally non-existent; yet when I explained the principle to you, you added one more level of attachment. If you want so much attachment, I have no way to teach you to understand the doctrine of the non-duality of emptiness and form. So you must wait until you look into it yourself and wake up to the principle. Perhaps then you will understand.

Although there are all kinds of form-dharmas, in general the form-skandha can be described in three broad classifications:

1) Form which can be seen and complemented, called complementary (*sapratigha*) and visible (*sanidarsana*).

2) Form which can be complemented but not seen, called complementary and invisible (*anidarsana*);

3) Form which can neither be seen nor complemented, called non-complementary (*apratigha*) and invisible.

The three kinds of form-dharmas are discriminated within the fields of the six objects of perception: sights, sounds, smells, tastes, objects of touch, and dharmas.

What are complementary, visible forms? They are dharmas which you can see and with which you can form a dharma-pair. People, self, other, and living beings; mountains, rivers, the great earth; and the ten thousand phenomena all have visible form, so they are all called complementary, visible dharmas, and are classified among the form-dharmas.

As to complementary, invisible forms, you can pair yourself with them, but you cannot see them. They include sounds, smells, tastes, and objects of touch, all of which can be complemented but not seen. For instance, to pair yourself with a sound which is an object of perception is to enter into a complementary relationship with what you hear: "Oh, this sounds good"; or, "That doesn't sound so good." You pair yourself with it and discriminations arise in the conscious mind, yet you are unable to see the sound. Tell me, what color is sound? Green, yellow, red, or white? It doesn't have a color. Well, then, is it square or round? Again you can't answer. No substantial visual appearance comes into being from the sound. Thus, the form-dharmas of this category are called complementary and invisible.

Sound is a kind of form that is an object of perception, that is, it belongs to the form-skandha of the five skandhas – form, feeling, cognition, formation, and consciousness. And so it is with smells. You can pair yourself with smells which are objects of perception and know that there is a certain fragrance, yet what does it look like? You cannot see it. Nevertheless, it still exists; but since it has no visible appearance, you are merely conscious of it; you recognize it without seeing it.

You use your tongue to taste; only the tongue can tell the palatable from the unpalatable. But do the five flavors – sour, sweet, bitter, hot, and salty – have a visible appearance? What do they look like? You cannot see them.

You cover your body with fine silks which are warm and comfortable. Their smooth touch on your skin gives you a very natural, happy feeling. What is the feeling like, the object of touch which is the object of perception? What visible appearance does it have? You can't see it. An object of touch which is the object of perception is also a complementary, invisible form which you can pair yourself with but cannot see.

Perhaps sights, sounds, smells, tastes, and objects of touch, the first five of the six objects of perception, have passed by, or perhaps they persist in your mind-consciousness, where they all leave a shadow. What is the shadow? Your eyes, for example, see a color, and your mind-consciousness knows, "What I just saw was red. I also saw yellow and green." Although the color has gone by, its trace remains in the mind-consciousness. Only its shadow is left. The same is true of sounds, smells, tastes, and objects of touch. Maintain that a certain phenomenon exists, and it has already gone past; maintain that it does not exist, yet you remember it. Although the objects of perception are no longer present, although the events are past and the feelings gone by, shadows are stored in the mind-consciousness, and these are called dharmas, the sixth of the six objects of perception. It belongs to the form skandha, but is classified as non-complementary and invisible, because as soon as you try to pair yourself with a dharma which is an object of perception, you find that it has already disappeared and no longer exists. You say that it doesn't exist, yet there in your mind-consciousness it still persists, as if it were carved on a wooden board. The shadow exists, but there is no way to see it, hear it, or seek out its genuine character. Thus the shadows of the first five objects of perception fall into the mind-consciousness and become non-complementary, invisible forms.

Feeling, Cognition, Formation & Consciousness

Sutra:

**So too are feeling, cognition, formation, and conscious-
ness. Shariputra, all dharmas are empty of characteristics.
They are not produced, not destroyed, not defiled, not pure,
and they neither increase nor diminish.**

Commentary:

The form-skandha is this way and **so too** are the other four
skandhas: **feeling, cognition, formation, and consciousness**. They
are of the same nature as form. Just as form does not differ from
emptiness, so too:

> *Feeling does not differ from emptiness;*
> *Emptiness does not differ from feeling.*
> *Feeling itself is emptiness;*
> *Emptiness itself is feeling.*
> *Cognition does not differ from emptiness;*
> *Emptiness does not differ from cognition.*
> *Cognition itself is emptiness;*
> *Emptiness itself is cognition.*
> *Formation does not differ from emptiness;*
> *Emptiness does not differ from formation.*
> *Formation itself is emptiness;*
> *Emptiness itself is formation.*

Consciousness does not differ from emptiness;
Emptiness does not differ from consciousness.
Consciousness itself is emptiness;
Emptiness itself is consciousness.

Therefore, the sutra text says, **so too are...** feeling, cognition, formation, and consciousness are the same as emptiness and form.

I have spoken about feeling, cognition, formation, and consciousness many times. From where do feeling, cognition, formation, and consciousness come, and to what place do feeling, cognition, formation, and consciousness go? Ultimately what are feeling, cognition, formation, and consciousness? We should understand what their substance is, for through understanding their substance, we will understand their function. When we understand their function, we will know how to defeat them. I will employ some rather superficial levels of reasoning to explain this.

What is **form**? The body is included among the form-dharmas; since it is form, it is called the "form-body". Your form-body has an appearance, but when you seek for its origin you will find that it is empty. This, too, I have explained many times. When the four great elements, namely earth, water, fire, and wind, unite, the body comes into being. This is what is meant by having a form. Working together, the elements establish a corporation. The corporation comes into being from the four conditioned causes: earth, which is characterized by solidity and durability; water, which is characterized by moisture; fire, which is characterized by warmth; wind, which is characterized by movement.

When the four conditioned causes disperse, each has a place to which it returns; therefore, the body becomes empty. As the sutra says, **form does not differ from emptiness; emptiness does not differ from form.**

Form does not differ from emptiness: this is true emptiness. **Emptiness does not differ from form**: this is wonderful existence. True emptiness is wonderful existence, and wonderful existence is true emptiness. It is not the case that outside true emptiness there is a separate wonderful existence; it is also not the case that moving wonderful existence to one side reveals true emptiness. What is true emptiness is just wonderful existence! What is wonderful existence is just true emptiness! Before the creation of the universe, before one's parents bore one, in the substance of the original face, the Buddha and living beings are not the slightest bit different. Thus the sutra says, **form does not differ from emptiness; emptiness does not differ from form**. The four great elements transform themselves and unite into a form-body, a corporeal body which has a visible appearance.

Once the body manifests, it likes pleasurable **feelings**. There are three kinds of feelings, which correspond to the three kinds of suffering:

> *Feelings of suffering;*
> *Feelings of happiness;*
> *Feelings which are characterized*
> *   by neither suffering nor happiness.*

Are you afraid of suffering? The more you fear suffering, the more suffering there is. So you reply, "I'm not afraid of suffering." Is the suffering diminished? Because you don't fear suffering, although the suffering is no less, it can be said that it does not exist. For if you do not fear suffering, then at its origin there is no suffering. If you are afraid of suffering, the more suffering there is, the more you are aware of it. The more you are aware of suffering, the more and more and more suffering there is.

When you experience the feeling of suffering, you feel that of all the people in the world you are the one who suffers most. Everything is felt to be suffering. I have a disciple who feels this way. When he lectures, he lectures on suffering. When he eats, he likes to eat bitter things. (In Chinese, the character *ku* 苦 means both "bitter" and "suffering.") But when it comes to doing work, he doesn't like suffering, and he's annoyed by hard work; he likes happy work. In this world happy work is rarely encountered, and if it is, it is simply the result of having suffered.

"Feelings of happiness" refer to all the kinds of pleasure. You feel that owning a car will make you happy, but after you buy the car, you want an airplane. When you own an airplane, you want to buy a sailboat, you want to take a rocket to the moon. But you get sick, and there are no doctors on the moon, so you die on the moon and become a moon-ghost. Is that being happy or is it suffering? You have become the "ghost in the moon." Happy feelings are a cause of suffering. Some say they are pleasurable, but they fill up your mind with bigger and bigger pieces of dirt.

You ask, "How can all those kinds of false thinking stop?" Should one have feelings which are characterized by neither happiness nor suffering? One could say, "I don't wish to suffer and I also don't wish to be happy; I just want to make it through one very ordinary life and forget it." Not bad. In this one life you can say that you broke even. You did business and didn't make a profit, but you didn't take a loss, either. You didn't make money, but you didn't lose any. The initial assets were fifty million and you still have fifty million. No gain and no loss: that is what is meant by feelings which are characterized by neither happiness nor suffering. But you wasted effort and did business in vain. You came into this world all confused, and you leave it all confused. Your wealth has not been well established and your accounts have been mismanaged. Consequently, this is called "coming and going in confusion." It earns more confusion, and there is no interest in it.

As for **cognition**, you certainly must have false thoughts if you want enjoyment. You can't be without it. "How can I think of a way to buy a car? How I can buy a beautiful home? How can I think of a way to buy a steamship? An airplane?" Your false thoughts fly back and forth and your hair turns white. Why? It turns white from false thinking. As soon as you begin false thinking, your hair starts turning white.

When you lie in your bed at night you have a thousand plans, as I've said before. Sometimes you get up early to act on them. Sometimes sleeping seems nice, and you just sleep. **Formation** is basically to act out karma, that is, to really act upon your false thinking. Now I will tell you about the five skandhas as they are found in your body.

1) The body is the form-skandha.

2) Once you have the form-skandha, you then have feelings of enjoyment and pleasure.

3) You want pleasure, and so you give rise to false thinking, which is cognition. How can I get what I want? How can I actually indulge in pleasure?

4) You have to go and do it; this is formation.

5) Acting requires a certain amount of wisdom, a consciousness which is a kind of small intelligence, about a hair's worth.

If you live in the "small-wisdom loft"[18], then you only take care of small-wisdom undertakings with your small wisdom, a small bit of wisdom in a small, small loft. Can there be any great development? No. No big business is done by the very small company in the very small loft.

You must have wisdom to help you actually carry out your plans. When you have a plan and actually put it into effect, then you can accomplish the aim of your false thinking and obtain the pleasure you sought. You then supply your body with what it needs and seeks. Your body achieves its aims. "Oh…enjoyment! Ahhh!" The enjoyment lasts about five minutes. Because of the excessive exertion, your blood vessels rupture and then death comes. You can say that the enjoyment didn't last long. What was it all about? It was just the five skandhas.

The five skandhas are just five ways of uniting, of working together to open a company. The company, once opened, opens again and again. Again and again. In a lecture on the *Sutra of the Past Vows of Earth Store Bodhisattva*, I explained it this way: the

---

[18.] This lecture series was given at the Buddhist Lecture Hall at 125 Waverly Place, San Francisco. This reference is to a portion of the BLH where students studied.

skandha-company grows everywhere like a wild vine which is never cut. Once opened, the Five Skandhas Corporation, Inc. always stays open, always feeling that there is hope. What hope? "Ah! This life I didn't make money, but wait until next life and I will be able to make some." Who can know whether there will be even less capital in the next life?

It's just like gambling. You expect to win money, but as soon as you pull the handle on the slot machine, the money falls down into the machine and the house wins. It didn't last long. At first you expected to win, but you lost. It is the same with your body, yet you gamble with it. Why do you want to gamble with it as if it were money? Because you haven't seen through it, you don't know that there are so many subtle, wonderful, and inconceivable states between heaven and earth. There are all these states, and yet you cannot move forward even a single step.

But there is one step that is even more esoteric, even more profound. What should you do? Just make the greed in your mind disappear. That is to neither make money nor lose it. That way you can preserve a little of your original share[19], in order to cultivate. That is what is called "returning to the original source". Then you can return home.

Verse:

> *Feeling, cognition, formation, and consciousness*
>   *are like emptiness and form.*
> *Again he calls,*
>   *"Shariputra, pay attention, listen!"*
> *"All dharmas are empty of characteristics,"*
>   *lacking a nature of their own.*
> *"Not produced, not destroyed,"*
>   *they silently pervade;*

[19.] *shou yi dian ben fen* 守一點本份. The phrase is also sometimes used to imply "mind your own business" or "be content with your own lot."

"Not defiled, not pure,"
they are separate from corrupting filth;
"They neither increase nor diminish" –
enlighten the dark and mysterious middle.
In the pure and deep ultimate silence,
all creation is transcended:
A sudden awakening to the original perfect fusion
of self and dharmas.

Commentary:

The three kinds of form – complementary, visible form; complementary, invisible form; and non-complementary, invisible form – were explained above. Encompassed by those three general classifications is the further distinction of eleven kinds of form-dharma. They are the five perceptual faculties[20] – the eyes, ears, nose, tongue, and body – and in addition, the six objects of perception – sights, sounds, smells, tastes, objects of touch, and dharmas. The five perceptual faculties pair themselves with the six perceptual objects. Taken together they comprise the eleven kinds of form-dharma, which are found within the three more general classifications of form.

To review, all the defiling phenomena in front of your eyes, all that has visible appearance, is complementary, visible form. The four kinds of form-dharma which are complementary and invisible are sounds, smells, tastes, and objects of touch. The "perceptual objects of the mind" – that is, dharmas – are also part of the form-dharma and are classified as non-complementary, invisible form. When you try to look at this kind of form, you see nothing and have no awareness of its presence, yet you know about it in your thoughts. In what sense can a perceptual object of the mind be called a form-dharma? The five perceptual objects which appear before you leave behind shadows in your mind. The shadow, or

---

[20] Chinese *gen* 根, literarily "roots."

perceptual objects of the mind – the mind-defilers – are also form, a kind of form which is inside mind-consciousness.

Form itself is emptiness, and feeling, thinking, action, and consciousness are also empty. They are the same as form, which is an object of perception. Where does the form which is an object of perception come from? The pairing of the six forms which are objects of perception with the six perceptual faculties produces the six consciousnesses, in which there arises discrimination of the form. The specific nature of each of the six perceptual faculties (i.e. the consciousness associated with each) – seeing, hearing, smelling, tasting, feeling, and knowing – is empty. Since the nature is empty and the form is manifest from the nature, form is also empty. In other words, in form there is emptiness. You do not have to leave form to find emptiness.

Now I shall talk about form and the seeing-nature. Which of the two would you say exists first? If form exists first, then how can it manifest when there is no seeing? If you say that seeing exists first, then where does the seeing-nature go when there is no form? So, if there is no form, the seeing-nature has no function. Therefore, both the seeing-nature and form are fundamentally empty. You should not give rise to a one-sided nature given to attachment and become attached to the idea that existence itself is existence and emptiness itself is emptiness. The original non-duality of emptiness and existence is true emptiness and wonderful existence giving birth to wonderful functioning. Some people who do not understand the Buddhadharma see emptiness and think that it is certainly empty; they see existence and think that it is certainly existent. Not understanding the principle of the non-duality of emptiness and existence, they seek outside themselves, they look for another head to put on top of the head they already have, and they get caught up in false thinking. When the Buddha spoke the *Heart Sutra*, he proclaimed the wonderful Dharma, the principle of the non-duality of emptiness and existence.

Feeling, cognition, formation, and consciousness are like emptiness and form. / Again he calls, "Shariputra, pay attention, listen!" / "All dharmas are empty of characteristics," lacking a nature of their own. The five skandhas – form, feeling, cognition, formation, and consciousness – are a general categorization of all dharmas, which can be further divided into the 100 dharmas: eleven form-dharmas (*rupa*), eight mind-dharmas (*citta*), fifty-one dharmas belonging to the mind (*caitasika*), twenty-four non-interacting dharmas (*citta viprayukta*), and six unconditioned dharmas (*asamskrta*).

The eleven form-dharmas, which were discussed above, refer to the pairing of the five perceptual faculties with the six perceptual objects. The eight mind-dharmas are these:

1) the eye-consciousness;
2) the ear-consciousness;
3) the nose-consciousness;
4) the tongue-consciousness;
5) the body-consciousness;
6) the mind-consciousness;
7) the defiling mind-consciousness (*manas*);
8) the storehouse-consciousness (*alaya*).

There are fifty-one dharmas belonging to the mind. They comprise the two skandhas of feeling and cognition. The skandha of formation consists of the twenty-four non-interacting dharmas. In addition there are the six unconditioned dharmas. Together they make 100 dharmas.

Maitreya Bodhisattva transformed all the teachings of Shakyamuni Buddha's lifetime into 660 categories of dharma. Since 660 categories were still too many, later on the Bodhisattvas Vasubandhu and Asanga summarized them into 100 dharmas.[21]

The verse says, "'All dharmas are empty of characteristics,' lacking a nature of their own." In other words, the five skandha-

---

[21] The 660 dharmas are explained in the *Yogacarabhumi-Sastra* (T. 1579). For the *Hundred Dharmas*, see the *bai fa ming men lun* 百法明門論.

dharmas – form, feeling, cognition, formation, and consciousness – are all empty. They have no nature of their own; their substance is empty.

"Not produced, not destroyed," they silently pervade. Nagarjuna Bodhisattva recited a verse of several lines which explains in detail the dharmas of production and extinction. How did he put it?

> *Birth in the past is not birth.*
> *Birth in the future is not birth either.*
> *Besides birth in the past and birth in future*
> *There is birth in the present, and that is no-birth.*

"Birth in the past is not birth." When birth has already taken place, how can there still be birth? Take, for example, a tree. Once a tree has sprouted, you cannot say it will sprout again.

"Birth in the future is not birth either." If there is no birth for the already-born, the not-yet-born has not been born either, has it? How can it have a birth if it still has not been born?

"Besides birth in the past and birth in the future / There is birth in the present, and that is no-birth." "There is birth in the present, and that is no-birth" is the same principle as "The past mind cannot be obtained, the present mind cannot be obtained, and the future mind cannot be obtained."[22] Thus Nagarjuna Bodhisattva made clear the doctrine of no production and no extinction. This expression of the theory is quite complete.

The Dharma spoken by the Buddha has eight characteristics:

> *No production and no extinction;*
> *No permanence and no annihilation;*
> *No unity and no differentiation;*
> *No coming and no going.*

[22.] *Vajra (Diamond) Sutra*

With his four-line verse, Nagarjuna Bodhisattva described birth; extinction can be described in the same way:

Extinction in the past is not extinction;
Extinction in the future is not extinction either.
Besides extinction in the past and
*   extinction in the future,*
There is extinction in the present,
*   and that is no-extinction.*

When such a doctrine is proclaimed, most people are not very clear about it. That is the reason I never talk about this kind of doctrine. Nevertheless, now I will talk about no production and no extinction.

"Not produced, not destroyed," they silently pervade. / "Not defiled, not pure," they are separate from corrupting filth. Our fundamental nature is without defilement or purity. But as soon as we are born and become people, there is defilement and purity. Yet the defilement and purity are **not defiled** and **not pure**. Nonetheless, as people, we have the kind of nature which is attached to accounting for things in a one-sided manner, and so we say, "This is defiled and that is pure." It is our attachment-nature which causes the change to defilement and purity.

How can we say that it is the way that our minds become attached? Take, for example, our hands. Sometimes, in particular circumstances, hands become smeared with various kinds of excrement: for instance, human excrement or pig's excrement. While your hands are smeared with it, you think they are very filthy. But once you have washed them off with water, you consider them clean. However, if you use a washcloth with excrement or some other impure substance on it, you still feel that it is unclean even after you have finished washing it with soap. You feel that if the washcloth has touched excrement or become smeared with it, you cannot get it clean, so you throw it out. Even though the washcloth has been washed, you always feel in your mind that it is not clean. But after people wash their hands with water, their minds are not attached in the same way. They don't talk about taking a knife and cutting off a hand to get rid of it, not wanting it because it is not clean. But why is the hand considered clean when the washcloth isn't? It's that you can't get rid of your hand, so your mind considers it clean. If it were not clean, you still could not give it up and throw it out. But even when the washcloth is washed clean, you don't want it. Nor do you wish to rub your face with it. As soon as you rubbed it on your face, you would feel that the stench had been rubbed into your face. Originally there was excrement wrapped in the washcloth, so in your mind you do not want it; it is too unclean. Yet it is all in your mind. If there is not that kind of attachment in your mind, then there is no defilement and no purity. When the attachment is made to disappear, the state is reached when "'Not defiled, not pure,' they are separate from corrupting filth."

If your mind does not have that kind of attachment, there is no problem. For even when there is filth, filth is just the same as purity. The original substance of one's own nature is neither defiled nor pure. Therefore, all is without characteristics and originally has no defilement or purity.

If you are capable of attaining the principle of the Way of neither defilement nor purity, so that your mind is not affected by defilement and purity, you will unite with your own nature; your virtue will equal that of heaven and earth, and your light, that of the sun and moon. How can the Buddha be like infinite suns? Because the Buddha was able to attain the principle of the Way of neither defilement nor purity. If you are capable of attaining this kind of natural principle of the Way, which is neither defiled nor pure, you and the four seasons – spring, summer, fall, and winter – have all been united and transformed into one. You can be united with the auspiciousness and misfortune of gods and ghosts. Why are you unable to accomplish this? Because you have the kind of nature which is attached to accounting for things in a one-sided manner. If you didn't, you could return to the original source and so leave defilement.

"They neither increase nor diminish" – enlighten the dark and mysterious middle. When you have attained enlightenment, there is neither increase nor decrease in your own nature. You have become enlightened to the most subtle and wonderful noumenal substance of the Middle Way. I spoke earlier about Nagarjuna Bodhisattva and the doctrine of non-production which he proclaimed. I also mentioned the dharma of the eight characteristics explained by the Buddha during the Vaipulya period.

> *No production and no extinction;*
> *No permanence and no annihilation;*
> *No unity and no differentiation;*
> *No coming and no going.*

Most people are attached either to annihilation or to permanence. Annihilation and permanence are the views of external paths, but the Dharma which was spoken by the Buddha is neither annihilationism nor eternalism; it is a dharma of neither unity nor differentiation.

Let's talk about us. Would you say that people are annihilated? When people die, do they then not exist? Or would you say that people live eternally? If so, then why don't we see any people from ancient times right now? We don't see them because people don't live forever. Would you say then that people do not live eternally? The rice which we now eat is the same rice which the ancients ate. The rice has not been annihilated. If you say that it has not been annihilated, you must say that it is eternal. The ancients are not eternal, but we are eternally eating the rice the ancients ate! Since we eat it, how is it still eternal? We eat it all the time! Therefore, the Dharma spoken by the Buddha is neither annihilationism nor eternalism. So you should not be attached either to a view of annihilationism or to a view of eternalism; you should unite instead with the Middle Way. And so the verse says, "enlighten the dark and mysterious middle."

"No coming and no going." The Buddha, the Thus Come One, does not come from anywhere or go anywhere. We should not only mention the Thus Come One, since we people also neither come nor go. You may say that there is a coming, but where do people come from? You don't know. You may say that there is a going; but when we die, where do we go? You don't know that either. "No coming and no going:" there is nowhere that we come from and nowhere that we go. In other words, there is neither unity nor differentiation. The lack of unity means there is no sameness, and the lack of differentiation means there are no two different characteristics. That is, there is no characteristic of commonality and no characteristic of distinction.

Would you say that there is a characteristic of commonality? Let's talk about the body. The body is not just composed of one kind of thing that is organized to become a body. There are many different divisions. That is what is meant by "no unity." And "no differentiation?" Generally speaking, the body is just a body. When there isn't any other distinction made, that is what is meant by "no differentiation". To explain this kind of principle is very complicated. One time a little is said and the next time a little is said. When it has been talked about several more times, you will be able to understand.

They neither increase nor diminish. One's own nature neither increases nor decreases.

In the pure and deep ultimate silence, all creation is transcended. Being very, very pure one transcends the creative and transformative processes of heaven and earth.

A sudden awakening to the original perfect fusion of self and dharmas. If you are able to understand simultaneously all the various principles which have been expounded, you will suddenly awaken to the fact that self and dharmas are originally perfectly fused, unobstructed, non-dual, and undifferentiated. Self and dharmas are one.

There is a Chinese saying which is very helpful in understanding that **they neither increase nor diminish**:

The years and months are unfeeling,
In increase is decrease.

One cannot say that the years and months have any human feelings at all. All that is mentioned is that their increasing is a decreasing. If it is said that there is neither increase nor decrease, how then is there increase and decrease nonetheless? What increases and decreases also neither increases nor decreases.

"The years and months are unfeeling." You say, "I don't want to go." You stand here today, wanting to stop the flow, saying, "Time, don't accompany me any further." You wish to tell it not to go past, but unless you make the sun stand still, no matter what you do, you will not stop it from flowing. Now, although science has made progress, it still has found no method capable of making the sun stand still. Therefore, time is unfeeling.

"In increase is decrease." This year we are sixty years old, and next year sixty-one years old. Although it may seem that our life-span has increased by one year, if you calculate toward the year of death... For instance, if I were to die at the age of 100 and had now lived to be sixty-one, there would still remain thirty-nine years. My life would have already decreased to thirty-nine years. Therefore, when one side increases, the other side decreases. "In increase is decrease." So also in decrease is increase. If you really understand this principle, you know that there is basically neither increase nor decrease. When I was teaching you Chinese, I said, "If you do not have an old heart, you have eternal youth." Therefore, "in increase is decrease."

What should be done?

Tasty Buddhadharma!
After the bitter, the sweet.

The Buddhadharma is really most flavorful. When you study the Buddhadharma, you study a little bit, and then you understand a little bit. Recently I said, "Regarding becoming enlightened, there are small enlightenments, there are middle-sized enlightenments, and there great enlightenments." How big is a small enlightenment? Perhaps it is as small as a speck of dust bordering on emptiness. In the field of your eighth consciousness, you have already had a small enlightenment and you still do not know it.

When you have a middle-sized enlightenment, you feel, "Ah, I understand a little more of the doctrine. That is what **neither increase nor diminish** is basically about! Fundamentally, **not produced, not destroyed, not defiled, not pure** has so many meanings!" You understand the meaning of those doctrines: that is middle-sized enlightenment.

Great enlightenment ends birth and death. You know how you come and how you go. You know what is meant by increase, by decrease, and by **not produced and not destroyed**. That's great enlightenment.

> *Tasty Buddhadharma!*
> *After the bitter, the sweet.*

First, you certainly must endure a little bit of suffering. That does not mean to study for three and a half days or even five days, and then to say, "I have studied enough Buddhadharma." No, you certainly should let go of that sort of patience; get rid of it, and say, "No matter what difficulty, I want to learn." This is why we stick to an unvarying schedule of language and sutra study. Unless there are special situations, I absolutely won't be lazy about teaching you. Why? It is just that you must reliably, truly cultivate, and then you can get to the flavor: "After the bitter, the sweet." You must first take the bitter, and afterwards you can obtain what is sweet. So in studying the Buddhadharma, no one should be afraid of suffering. Don't be afraid. The more suffering, the better. You should get up your energy, firm your stance, direct your will, and go forward with vigor and valor. You shouldn't be afraid of suffering; you shouldn't be afraid of difficulty! Then you can study the Buddhadharma.

The Emptiness of the Eighteen Fields

Sutra:

Therefore, in emptiness there is no form, feeling, cognition, formation, or consciousness; no eyes, ears, nose, tongue, body, or mind; no sights, sounds, smells, tastes, objects of touch, or dharmas; no field of the eyes, up to and including no field of mind-consciousness.

Verse:

> *Therefore in emptiness*
> *   there are no characteristics of form.*
> *Feeling, cognition, formation, and consciousness*
> *   disappear also,*
> *As well as the six faculties and six objects,*
> *   together with six consciousnesses.*
> *With three minds in three ceasings,*
> *   three closures are passed through.*
> *The great cart of the white ox turns*
> *   with the sound lin-lin.*
> *A little yellow-faced child jumps and thumps*
> *   in agitation.*
> *What instructive meaning is there in this?*
> *The front double-three and the back double-three meet.*

Commentary:

Therefore, in emptiness there is no form. This sentence refers back to an earlier passage in the sutra: **Not produced, not destroyed, not defiled, not pure, and they neither increase nor diminish.** Since that is the case, in emptiness – true emptiness – there is no form.

No... feeling, cognition, formation, or consciousness. Their basic substance is also empty.

No eyes, ears, nose, tongue, body, or mind. None of the six perceptual faculties exist.

No sights, sounds, smells, tastes, objects of touch, or dharmas. The six objects of perception do not exist either.

No field of the eyes, up to and including no field of mind-consciousness. All the six consciousnesses are also empty.

The *Heart Sutra* speaks about the true emptiness of prajna. The true emptiness of prajna is wonderful existence. Wonderful existence is no existence; it is true emptiness. Therefore, it is said, "True emptiness does not obstruct wonderful existence, and wonderful existence does not obstruct true emptiness. True emptiness is wonderful existence, and wonderful existence is true emptiness."

Earlier the sutra says, **form does not differ from emptiness; emptiness does not differ from form.** The form-dharma of the five skandhas is empty. The five skandha-dharmas are a summation of dharmas in general, and the others – the six perceptual faculties, the six objects of perception, and the six consciousnesses – are special characteristics of dharmas. Since the characteristics of their summation are empty, their special characteristics must be non-existent also. Therefore the sutra says there are **no eyes, ears, nose, tongue, body, or mind; no sights, sounds, smells, tastes, objects of touch, or dharmas; no field of the eyes, up to and including no field of mind-consciousness.**

The six objects of perception, the six perceptual faculties, and the six consciousnesses are together called the eighteen fields. The six perceptual faculties together with the six objects of perception are called the twelve dwellings. The six perceptual faculties are also called the six entrances. There are five skandhas, six perceptual faculties, twelve dwellings, and eighteen fields. The six faculties, six objects, and six consciousnesses, which together comprise the eighteen fields, are all empty also. They do not exist either.

"Why talk about all these dharmas if they do not exist?" you ask. They exist among common people, but not where there are sages who have been certified as having attained enlightenment.

The verse says, *Therefore, in emptiness there are no characteristics of form.* Because this principle was stated in the opening paragraph of the sutra, the sutra text now says, **therefore, in emptiness there is no form**.

The verse continues, *Feeling, cognition, formation, and consciousness disappear also.* They too are empty, non-existent.

As well as the six faculties and six objects, together with six consciousnesses. The six perceptual faculties are the eyes, ears, nose, tongue, body, and mind. Sights, sounds, smells, tastes, objects of touch, and dharmas are the six objects of perception; they appear as the complement of the six faculties. In Chinese, the word *gen* 根, "root," is used for the six perceptual faculties, conveying the idea of growth, while the word *chen* 塵, "dust," is used for the six objects of perception, conveying the idea of defiling or defilement.

Between the six faculties and the six objects are produced discriminations which are called the six consciousnesses: the eye-consciousness, ear-consciousness, nose-consciousness, tongue-consciousness, body-consciousness, and mind-consciousness. Those six consciousnesses, the six perceptual faculties, and the six objects of perception are together called the eighteen fields.

With three minds in three ceasings, three closures are passed through. The three minds are the minds of past, present, and future. The mind of the past must cease, and the minds of the present and future must cease as well. Because you don't want to have three minds and three ceasings, it is said, "The mind of the past cannot be obtained, the mind of the present cannot be obtained, and the mind of the future cannot be obtained." None of the three minds can be obtained.

Three closures are passed through. If one is capable of not having the mind of the past arise, of not having the mind of the present be produced, and of not having the mind of the future come into being, then one does not think of good or of evil. When the three minds do not exist, how can one think of good or evil? When through your vigorous cultivation you reach the state of taking dhyana-joy as food and you are filled with Dharma-bliss, then by sitting quietly and properly you can open your first, middle, and top closures[23]. The first closure is called the "closure of the tail," the middle one is called the "closure of the spine," and the top one is called either the "jade-pillow closure" or the "old door of birth and death." The first and second closures are easy to break through. When you reach the third closure, you encounter a bit of difficulty.

What kind of situation do you encounter after you pass through the third closure and still continue to cultivate? Then what do you experience?

The great cart of the white ox turns with the sound lin-lin. The *Wonderful Dharma Lotus Flower Sutra* calls the Buddha-Vehicle the great cart of the white ox. "There is only the Buddha-Vehicle; there are no other vehicles."[24] After you have realized Buddhahood, but not before, you can go along the road in this great carriage. In other words, we work hard to be able to turn the Dharma wheel to teach and transform living beings.

[23.] Chinese *guan* 關, "closure" or "gate."

Why does the *Wonderful Dharma Lotus Flower Sutra* call it the great cart of the white ox and not the great cart of the black or the yellow ox, or the great many-colored ox? The whiteness of the ox represents the non-defilement of our own nature. Thus, when you practice, the Great-Vehicle Dharma "turns with the sound of *lin-lin*." As it goes along on the road, this great vehicle, the carriage of the white ox, makes the sound *lin-lin*, the sound a cart makes going along a road.

At that point in the cultivation of the Way, everyone experiences a certain feeling; you feel like you're drunk, like you're asleep, and also like you're dreaming. In the last analysis you don't know whether it is true or false, empty or real. Your four limbs are especially soft; your hands and legs feel like soft mud. They have no strength and don't want to do anything at all. But when you sit, or perhaps when you are not meditating, your heart constantly thumps.

It's not your heart that's thumping, but your spleen. When you are walking along and feel "bung, bung, bung," you presume it's your heart thumping, but it's the spleen. When you run fast, the spleen has to work a little harder, so it thumps and hits your stomach to aid your stomach in digesting. Therefore, the verse speaks next of *a little yellow-faced child who jumps and thumps in agitation.*

Who is the yellow-faced child? He is simply the thoughts in your mind. The seat of the mind is the spleen, which is yellow[25], so it is called the "little yellow-faced child." It jumps back and forth,

---

24. The quotation is from the *Analogies Chapter* of the *Wonderful Dharma Lotus Flower Sutra*, in which the Buddha presents the parable of a man of great power whose huge mansion catches fire. His children, intent upon their games, will not leave the dwelling. The man lures them out of the burning house by telling them that outside are three kinds of carriage for them to play with: one goat-drawn, one deer-drawn, and one ox-drawn. But when the children escape to safety, each is given the same kind of carriage, magnificent beyond his wildest dreams and drawn by a great white ox. Thus the Buddha uses expedient vehicles to lure living beings to the real doctrine, that of the one Buddha-Vehicle Dharma.

and when that happens to people when they meditate, they think to themselves, "Oh! My heart is really pounding a lot. Maybe I have heart trouble!" and they become afraid. But they haven't contracted heart trouble, so there's no need to be afraid. This condition is a result of cultivating the Way. Your heart also feels like it is pounding when you're afraid, like a rabbit jumping up and down or thumping. When the great cart of the white ox turns the Dharma wheel, the thoughts in the mind thump, thump, thump ferociously, just as when you are afraid. But it is only a little yellow-faced child jumping and thumping in agitation.

What instructive meaning is there in this? If you were to ask what this is about, what kind of principle of the Way it is, what its purpose and intent is…

The front double-three and the back double-three meet. In front and in back there are three places. At that time, the roads of birth and death meet. Before, each had taken its own road; birth went down the road of birth, and death went down the road of death. The road of birth and the road of death were not the same. Now birth and death are one. Birth is death and death is birth. It is the same as **form does not differ from emptiness; emptiness does not differ from form. Form itself is emptiness; emptiness itself is form**. That is to say, birth and death are non-dual. Or in other words, there is no birth and no death. But you must work hard. If you don't work hard, if you go forward one step and retreat four steps, it is still of no use. Unless you don't want to cultivate, you should go forward and make progress every day; you should be vigorous. As soon as you retreat, the work you have done before is wasted; it is lost. Then, if you still wish to return to the original source, you must start over from the beginning. So in cultivating, you can only go vigorously forward; you cannot retreat.

[25.] According to Chinese cosmology, the color yellow represents the earth (*tu* 土). The earth is controlled by the spleen (*pi* 脾), which is the seat of the mind (*yi* 意). Chinese medicine teaches that the function of the spleen is to beat or thump on the stomach in order to aid digestion. Thus the analogy.

The Twelve Conditioned Causes

Sutra:

And no ignorance or ending of ignorance, up to and including no old age and death or ending of old age and death.

Commentary:

This passage mentions the twelve conditioned causes (*pratitya-samutpada*), which those of the Condition-Enlightened Vehicle (*pratyekabuddhas*) cultivate. The twelve conditioned causes help people be born and die and be reborn again. The Condition-Enlightened cultivate the twelve dharmas of conditioned cause, and, understanding the principles of human life, they become enlightened and are certified as having attained the fruition of Pratyekabuddhahood. They are called those of the middle vehicle. Hearers (*shravakas*) are the small vehicle, Pratyekabuddhas are the middle vehicle, and Bodhisattvas are the great vehicle.

What is **ignorance**?

1) Ignorance is the lack of understanding. In everyday language it is called being mixed-up. It means that you have not understood the principle.

2) Because you are so mixed up and you do not understand, your behavior is mixed up, your actions are false. By false activity is meant doing what you shouldn't do. The false activity leads to…

3) Empty and false recognition, that is, consciousness.

4) Mixed-up name and form follow.

5) Then there are mixed-up entrances; the six entrances come into being. From mixed-up entrances there arises,

6) Mixed-up contact. When there is mixed-up contact, one thinks of,

7) Mixed-up enjoyment. From such mixed-up feeling comes,

8) Mixed-up love, that is, craving. From mixed-up love there then arises,

9) Mixed-up seeking and grasping, which is followed by,

10) Mixed-up having – that is, existence. To have is to obtain. From mixed-up having, one can then obtain,

11) Future birth. And from rebirth comes,

12) Old age and death.

These are the twelve conditioned causes, and they all begin with being mixed up. Because they are mixed up in the beginning, they are mixed up at the conclusion. You pass through one mixed-up life to the next, and that next life is also mixed up. The twelve conditioned causes are all mixed up, and mixed-up conditioned causes are exactly what ordinary people are unable to understand.

From the very beginning, the twelve conditioned causes are mixed up. The desires that people give rise to, whether for food or for sex, are all produced from ignorance, the first of the conditioned causes. Ignorance is just another name for being mixed up. When thoughts arise, there follows a desire to act, to go and do it – the second of the conditioned causes. In this way, the twelve conditioned causes explain the principles of how we are born and how we die. Because there is ignorance, there is sexual behavior. The mixed-up sexual behavior is produced from the state of being mixed up. When the mixed-up behavior exists, there arises a mixed-up recognition, a mixed-up discrimination, a consciousness, the third conditioned cause. This is the body of the intermediate skandha-consciousness (*antarabhava*). When a man and woman indulge in sexual behavior, if an intermediate skandha-consciousness has an appropriate interpersonal causal connection with that mother and father, then even if it is a thousand or ten thousand miles away, and even if only the tiniest thread of light is emitted, it sees the light and goes there to become a foetus.

When the foetus comes into being, there is name and form, the fourth conditioned cause. Name refers to the four skandhas of feeling, cognition, formation, and consciousness, while form refers to the form-skandha. Four kinds of awareness – feeling, cognition, formation, and consciousness – exist in the mother's belly in name only; they have not yet actually come into being. Once name and form come to exist, there are then six entrances, the fifth conditioned cause. These are six perceptual faculties as they give rise to the seeing-nature, the hearing-nature, the smelling-nature, the tasting-nature, the touching-nature, and the knowing-nature. Those six natures are called the six entrances. Once the six entrances exist, the child becomes aware of contact, the sixth conditioned cause. Therefore, it is said, "The six entrances lead to contact." Having awareness of contact, the child becomes receptive to feelings, the seventh conditioned cause, and from that the eighth, love, is produced in the heart. Only after love is born does the child wish to seek and grasp; this is the ninth conditioned cause. Therefore, "love leads to grasping," seeking and grasping for what one loves. Thereupon one wants to have, to get for oneself; this is the tenth conditioned cause. Because of thinking and getting, there is rebirth in the next life; after rebirth comes old age and death, the twelfth and last conditioned cause.

If there were no ignorance, there would be no activity. This is the extinguishing cycle of the twelve conditioned causes.

> *When ignorance is ended, activity is ended.*
> *When activity is ended, consciousness is ended.*
> *When consciousness is ended, name and form are ended.*
> *When name and form are ended,*

the six entrances are ended.
When the six entrances are ended, contact is ended.
When contact is ended, then enjoyment –
    that is, feeling – is ended.
When enjoyment is ended, love is ended.
When love is ended, grasping is ended.
When grasping is ended, having is also ended.
When having is ended,
    birth, old age, and death are ended.

Verse:

No ending of ignorance –
    its basic nature is empty.
False activity, discrimination,
    followed by name and form;
The six entrances,
    contact, feeling, love, grasping, having;
Rebirth, and old age and death are each that way too.
For ten thousand miles the sky is clear,
    without a cloud or a shadow;
Still water fills a deep pool
    and reveals the light of the moon.
Like people who drink when thirsty
    and know the hot from the cold,
Talking about food, and helping it grow:
    the work is always wanting.

Commentary:

No ending of ignorance – its basic nature is empty. That is, ignorance does not exist.

False activity, discrimination, followed by name and form. The verse says that after discrimination comes name and form; after name and form come the six entrances; after the six entrances, contact; after contact, enjoyment. Enjoyment, then love; love, then grasping; grasping, then having; from having come rebirth and old age and death. Therefore, the verse says, *The six entrances, contact, feeling, love, grasping, having; / Rebirth, and old age and death are each that way too.* They are all connected together in the twelve conditioned causes. When the time comes that they all do not exist, it is like a cloudless sky. *For ten thousand miles the sky is clear, without a cloud or a shadow.*

Still water fills a deep pool and reveals the light of the moon. It is also like the bright moon appearing as a reflection in clear water.

Like people who drink when thirsty and know the hot from the cold. Having the spiritual skill, the *gong fu,* of knowing and being enlightened to the twelve dharmas of conditioned cause is compared to drinking water, because when you are thirsty and drink, you yourself know whether the water is cold or warm.

Talking about food and helping it grow: the work is always wanting. If you yourself don't actually cultivate, if you don't look into the twelve conditioned causes and become enlightened to them and say, "Oh, the twelve conditioned causes are empty, empty, empty!" – if you haven't done these things but you talk endlessly about emptiness without having genuinely obtained its real meaning and principle for yourself, then it is a case of merely "talking about food" but not eating it. As it says in the *Shurangama Sutra,* "In the end, talking about food cannot make you full."

"Helping it grow" refers to the extremely stupid people of the country of Song in ancient China. In those days, when you wanted to refer to a country where the people were stupid, you said, "Like the people of Song," since they were the stupidest. Just how stupid were they?

Among the men of Song there was someone who felt sorry for his plants and pulled them up.

He was worried that the grain he had planted wouldn't grow, so, saying, "Ah, my seedlings are growing so slowly," he pulled them up to help them grow. He pulled them up so they were one or two inches taller and said, "You see, they grew two inches today."

Having arrived in a dull hurry.

He was muddled and confused, and had the appearance of great weariness. He arrived home panting and exclaimed, "Too much bitter suffering, too much bitter suffering!" and he said to his family,

"Today I am very tired."

"Today I feel so tired that I'm sick, because I did so much work. I helped the plants to grow." His son went running to see them. His son said, "Ah, my father has such great ability, so much divine psychic power that he can help the plants grow. Heaven and earth help the plants grow, but the amount they help in any one day is infinitesimal. What mantra did he recite to help the plants grow?" And he ran off to the fields to look.

As to the plants, they had withered.

They'd all dried up; they were dead.

This is just to say that in cultivating the Way you should not think, "Ah, I have become enlightened! I have become enlightened! I have become enlightened!" Or, "Ah, how is it that I have still not become enlightened. How should I be so that I will get enlightened? This way I don't get enlightened, and that way I don't get enlightened. I go forward several steps and haven't been enlightened yet; I retreat several steps and have not been enlightened either. I jump several jumps and don't get enlightened. I sat for one whole hour and still have not become enlightened. After all, how do you get enlightened?"

If you have a mind like that, you will never be able to become enlightened. Why? Because in your mind your thoughts of wanting to become enlightened press down on your potential for enlightenment in much the same way as the man from Song who helped his plants to grow. Therefore, the verse says, "Talking about food, and helping things grow: the work is always wanting." In short, there is never any merit in it.

You yourself must cultivate with energy and with a level mind. You must put your feet down diligently on the actual ground. You should not say, "Will I be able to get enlightened tomorrow? Will I be able to get enlightened the day after? When will I be able to become enlightened?" Don't cherish such thoughts, because the false-thinking mind is precisely what will cause your enlighten-ment to run away in fright. Your enlightenment is afraid of false thinking. So when you have false thinking, enlightenment just runs away. Why does your heart jump? Because it is afraid of your false thinking. It is also afraid of becoming enlightened. Since you want to become enlightened, your heart jumps and thumps, "Incredible! He wants to become enlightened!" So when your heart starts pounding, your karmic obstacles become afraid and imperceptibly think, "If he becomes enlightened, what will we do?" There won't be anything they can do.

Emptying the Four Truths

Sutra:

There is no suffering, no accumulating, no extinction, no Way.

Verse:

> *Each of the sufferings exerts pressure,*
>   *and all attack together,*
> *Accumulating is feelings which beckon,*
>   *each unlike the other.*
> *Only through extinction can the ultimate joy*
>   *be attained.*
> *Therefore, this is the Way that should be practiced*
>   *to awaken to the emptiness of dharmas.*
> *Through three turnings of the Four Truths*
>   *the Dharma wheel revolves,*
> *Seven shares in enlightenment,*
>   *the Eightfold Upright Path,*
>   *intention, mindfulness, and diligence.*
> *One day connect right through*
>   *and ripen the fruit of sagehood;*
> *Partial truth with residue is just a conjured city.*

Commentary:

This passage of the sutra empties the Four Truths: **suffering, accumulating, extinction,** and the **Way**. Those are the dharmas cultivated by the Hearers (*shravakas*). Why are they called Hearers? "Upon hearing the sound of the Buddha, they were enlightened to the Way." At the very beginning, the Buddha taught living beings who had causal connections with the kind of opportunity for change which is offered by the small vehicle.

When Shakyamuni Buddha first realized Buddhahood, he spoke the *Avatamsaka Sutra*. Though they had eyes, those of the two vehicles did not see; though they had ears, they did not hear. Why didn't they see? Because that kind of Dharma was too wonderful, too high, and too great. Because it is so wonderful, those of the two vehicles basically don't understand it. They don't know what is called the inconceivable. They were all like little children, and the ten-thousand-foot high *nisyanda*[26] body which was manifested by Shakyamuni Buddha was too high for them to see. So it was said:

> *The more I strain my gaze up towards it, the higher it soars. The deeper I bore down into it, the harder it becomes. I see it in front, but suddenly it is behind.*

You see something in front of you, and suddenly it is behind you. For instance, one of my disciples is now about to obtain the psychic power of the heavenly eye. He sometimes sees things before him which suddenly run around behind him, and he thinks, "At first the light was coming from behind, but now it is coming from in front. There was a light coming from the left, but then it went to the right." It is like when Shakyamuni Buddha emitted light to the left, and Ananda looked to the left; he emitted light to the right, and Ananda looked to the right, as the *Shurangama Sutra* relates. Because this Dharma is inconceivable, those of the two vehicles

---

[26.] Probable reconstruction of *lu she na* 盧舍那. The term is roughly equivalent to *sambhogakaya*, the "reward" or "enjoyment" body of the Buddha.

have no way to deal with it and no way to understand it fully. Although they have ears, they do not hear the perfect, sudden teaching. Because it is too profound, they do not understand it.

Thereupon, Shakyamuni Buddha, concealing the great and revealing the small, appeared in the body of a sixteen-foot-tall old bhikshu and spoke the dharma of the Four Truths (*catur-arya-satyani*): suffering (*duhkha*), accumulating (*samudaga*), extinction (*nirodha*), and the Way (*marga*).

There are three turnings of the Dharma wheel of the Four Truths, so called because they are like the revolving backwards and forwards of the wheel of the six paths. The first turning of the Dharma wheel of the Four Truths is the turning by manifestation; the second is the turning by exhortation, which urges you to study this dharma, and the third is the turning by verification.

The turning by manifestation runs this way: "This is suffering; its nature is oppression. This is accumulating; its nature is feeling which beckons. This is extinction; its nature is that it can be verified. This is the Way; its nature is that it can be cultivated."

The turning by exhortation runs this way: "This is suffering; you should know about it. This is accumulating; you should cut it off. This is extinction; you should verify it. This is the Way; you should cultivate it."

The turning verification runs as follows: "This is suffering; you should know about it. I already know about suffering and have no need to know more about it. In other words, now it is you who should know about suffering. For me to know about it again would be to add a head on top of a head. Second, this is accumulating; you should cut it off. I have already cut it off and need not cut it off again. Now it is I who am telling you to cut it off, and I am just waiting for you to do so. Third, this is extinction; you should verify it. I have already verified extinction, that is, the happiness of nirvana. I am just waiting for you to verify it. Fourth, this is the Way; you should cultivate it. I have already cultivated it and need not cultivate it further." The turning by verification attests that he himself has already reached attainment, and he tells you to cultivate. If he had no attainment, there would be no need for him to teach you to cultivate.

You say, "What suffering should I know about?" **Suffering** is the first of the Four Truths. Would you say that it is real? Suffering is real, as one of my disciples told her "guest-defiler" – her boyfriend. "Hurry up and go away, guest-defiler! I am suffering too much! If you don't go, I will suffer too much." "Guest-defiler" is a way of referring to an object of perception, and so this is a case of appearing in a body to speak the Dharma. This kind of phenomenon really exists. If the guest-defiler doesn't go you will suffer. Wouldn't you say that's strange? The guest-defiler goes, making it possible for the suffering to decrease.

There are three kinds of suffering: the suffering of suffering itself; the suffering of decay; and the suffering of the activity of the five skandhas. There are also the eight kinds of suffering, of which the first four are produced from your own body: the suffering of birth, the suffering of sickness, the suffering of old age, and the suffering of death. The second four kinds of suffering are caused by external situations: the suffering of being apart from those you love, the suffering of being together with those you detest, the suffering of not obtaining what you seek, and the suffering of the flourishing of the five skandhas. Then there are all the infinite kinds of suffering. The truth of suffering includes a lot of suffering.

Sufferings oppress people until they can't breathe. The sufferings press down and cut off the breath[27] until it is unbearable. "Guest-defiler, go away fast, fast! I am suffering too much." That is the truth of suffering. I have spoken about it a good deal before, so I need not speak about it in detail now.

Suffering is piled upon suffering: this is the truth of accumulating. *Each of the sufferings exerts pressure, and all attack together.* The three sufferings, the eight sufferings, and all the

---

27. *qi* 氣

infinite sufferings press down on you so that you can't breathe, all attacking you at once as if they were fighting with you. The guest-defiler comes, everything comes, grabbing a little here, grabbing a little there. The six consciousnesses and the six objects of perception and every kind of situation come from outside to attack you. Therefore, the verse says, "Each of the sufferings exert pressure, and all attack together." Each kind of suffering attacks you, and each is too much suffering. Suffering is added upon suffering.

Accumulating is feelings which beckon, each unlike the other. What accumulates is affliction. Afflictions are even more terrible than guest-defilers. Guest-defilers can only give you a little external provocation, but they also make afflictions attack from the inside. When the attack of the guest-defilers is carried to the inside, afflictions are generated.

Why is there affliction? The host-defiler moves as well. At first you were the host, that is, the one in charge, but now you are shaken so badly by the guest-defilers that you no longer know that you are the host. Then you lose your temper, and there is affliction. You can tell a guest-defiler to go away and you can push it aside, but you can't push the host-defiler anywhere, because it is already in your home. It is extremely fierce, much fiercer than the guest-defilers.

Affliction is the thing I want to talk about least, because I'm afraid that by talking about it, I will make you have even more afflictions. Before I say anything, you won't know how many afflictions there are and you can still not understand them. You can be afflicted without caring about it; unknowing and unaware, you let them go by. If I speak about them clearly, you will ask, "Which affliction is this, and which one is that?" Then you will add affliction to affliction. This is why I have lectured on sutras for such a long time without talking about how many afflictions there are.

You say, "Oh, I've heard you talk about them. Haven't you said that there are 84,000 kinds of affliction?" Not bad. Yes, there are

84,000 kinds of affliction; still, 84,000 kinds of affliction are too many to name one by one. I want to tell you the names of the afflictions now. The time has come.

The twenty subsidiary afflictions[28], derive their names from the fact that they follow you and me. If you have afflictions, they go along with you; if I have them, they go along with me; if others have them, they go along with others. Among the twenty subsidiary afflictions are ten small afflictions, two middle-sized afflictions, and eight large afflictions.

These are the ten small afflictions:

1) *Upset.* The mind loses its equanimity. Wouldn't you say that is an affliction? It is to be truly, totally, despicably messed up. Do you like the first one or not? If you like it, then take it.

2) *Enmity.* "I hate you; I hate you right through." Hate is the other side of love. Why do you hate people? It is because you love them and your love is unrequited. I have a disciple who had a guest-defiler of a boyfriend. As soon as he heard that she wanted to leave the home-life, his hatred arose, and he said to her on the telephone, "I hate you!" He really surprised and frightened her, and she said, "Oh, that is really terrible!"

3) The third, *annoyance*, is even fiercer than enmity. When you are annoyed, you are not at all at ease (*zi zai* 自在). The Chinese character for "annoyance" (*nao* 惱) is related to the word for brain (*nao* 腦), that is, your head. As soon as you become annoyed, your head hurts and your eyes burn. You can't tell how big your head is. The more you are disturbed, the bigger your head gets, and when you are extremely disturbed, you get water on the brain. That can be fatal. Your head swells up, bigger and bigger, until it is as big as it can get, and then the water pours out of your head and you die.

The Chinese word *nao* 惱, "annoyance," is used in the compound *fan nao* 煩惱, which means affliction.

---

28. *sui fan nao* 隨煩惱, "afflictions that follow"

4) *Repression*. The literal meaning is "to cover", as "Heaven covers over and Earth contains." Repression is even more harmful than upset, enmity, and annoyance, which are all externalized. Repression, on the other hand, implies a wish that others will not know. To cover up and to hide something inside is very harmful to you. It gives you ulcers. Americans don't get them as much as Chinese people, especially those who have left the home-life. Why? Because they repress their afflictions and do not let others know, and no one asks them about it. It isn't important, but they hide it inside; they are very clearly afflicted, but they cover it up so it cannot flow out. So inside they get ulcers. When people have this type of illness, you know they are repressing afflictions.

5) *Lying*. The Chinese character *huang* 謊, "lying", is made up of two characters, *yan* 言, "speech", and *huang* 荒, "crazy". False speech becomes an affliction. When you are upset, someone may ask you, "Why are you afflicted?" and you reply, "I'm not afflicted. Who's afflicted?" You even ask, "Who's afflicted?" The fire of ignorance inside you attacks and destroys even the heavens. Asked again, you still deny any affliction and say, "Who's afflicted?" That is the fifth affliction, lying.

I didn't want to tell you about that affliction, because I was afraid that when the time came to speak falsely, you might be like a certain one of my disciples. Now if he were to get angry, I might ask if he is angry, and he might say, "No, no, I didn't get angry." Then he would be lying. First, he would repress his anger, and then he would speak falsely. Because he didn't understand the method before, I would have kept him from lying by not explaining it. But now I have already talked about it.

6) *Obsequious flattery*. In your heart you simply don't like someone, but when you see him, you still want to speak to him nicely. The colloquial Chinese expression "to pat the horse" refers to this sort of flattery. When someone who is poor sees someone who is rich, he is particularly likely to say, "Aaah, Mr. Chaang, where are you gooooing?" – all in that tone of voice. His manner is

one of constant obsequious flattery. He pats you on the shoulder and laughs in an ugly way.

7) *Arrogance* is the seventh small affliction. "I won't even pay any attention to you. If you are rich, that's your affair. I'll just attend to whatever I have to do. See how big I am; I am Number One in the whole world. My body is even bigger than Mount Sumeru, so why do I have to be polite to you?" That kind of arrogance makes you think that your body is bigger than Mount Sumeru. The previous affliction of obsequious flattery is changed into arrogance. "You pat the horse, so I don't pay any attention to anyone."

8) Next comes *malevolence*. "So you are rich and powerful? Ha! I'll knife you to death, and then we will see of what use it will be." Here someone wishes to harm people, but doesn't actually do the harmful deeds. Thinking in your mind about harming people is what is called malevolence, your very own eighth small affliction.

9) *Jealousy*. I haven't given you this ninth small affliction before, but you've all had it for a long time. I don't know where you stole it from. It's jealousy. You are jealous of him, and he is jealous of you. Since you don't understand where the jealousy came from, I said that you stole it. Not understanding how it came about is the same as its being stolen. Since you didn't know, I'm telling you that your jealousy came from the list of ten small subsidiary afflictions.

10) The tenth, *stinginess*, is just about the same. Some people have it, and some people don't. Stinginess means that you cannot bear to give things up. You cannot stand giving. Although you have a penny, you clutch it in your palm and squeeze and squeeze and squeeze until it turns to water. Then you cry, "Oh, my penny has disappeared! I didn't even spend it, so where did it go?" The fact is that it turned to water. Stinginess, is the tenth affliction.

The two middle-sized subsidiary afflictions are *lack of shame* and *lack of humility*. The Chinese character *can* 慚, "shame" is composed of the element *xin* 心, meaning "mind" and the character *zhan* 斬, which means "to behead" or, more generally, "to cut off" or "to kill," as in the expression to "cut off affliction." When you are afflicted in your mind by a lack of shame, then if you do something wrong you don't admit it is wrong, and you do not know how to change and repent.

The lack of shame also refers to the failure to cut off the afflictions in your mind which should be cut off. Having a murderous intent in your mind which is left unrectified is also known as shamelessness. Since you lack shame, you know no embarrassment. Your actions are so lacking in light and uprightness that you ought to be unable to look at people; nevertheless, you do not even admit to being wrong. You still say, "What difference does it make? So-and-so acts wrongly in just the same way." You try to convince yourself that you are being reasonable, so you act as your own defense attorney. You say, "Because of this and that circumstance, I had a good cause to do what I did, and so I am right. Yes, because my reasoning is especially precise, I am confident that I am in the right."

What is meant by a lack of humility? The Chinese character *kui* 愧, translated as "humility" or "remorse" is written with an element meaning heart on the left and the character for ghost on the right. In other words, there is no light in your heart, but you nevertheless consider it right to have no light. That is to lack humility. Although you have a bad conscience and feel that you should apologize to other people, you still don't say "I'm sorry," but think to yourself, "I'm not going to apologize to those people!"

Next are the eight large subsidiary afflictions.

1) The first is *disbelief.* You never would have thought that the lack of belief is an affliction, would you? Someone afflicted by disbelief doesn't believe anything you say, no matter what it is, whether it is right or wrong. If you speak so that "heavenly flowers fall this way and that and golden lotuses spring forth from the earth,"[29] he still acts as if he didn't hear. If you explain something that contains the principles of the Way, he doesn't believe it. If you explain something that is unprincipled, he believes that even less.

You explain a little more, you explain a little less, in either case he doesn't believe it. If you talk about existence, or nothingness, or emptiness, or non-emptiness, he won't believe any of it. In short, the essential tenet of his principles is disbelief.

2) The second of the large subsidiary afflictions is *torpor*. None of you thought that torpor was one of the large subsidiary afflictions. To be torpid is not to study the dharma-doors diligently. A person afflicted by torpor is always torpid, whatever he does. He eats lazily, waiting five minutes between mouthfuls. When he sleeps, he is in a stupor. The only time he is energetic is when he plays mahjong. This affliction makes one lazy about the Dharma and lazy in cultivation. The laziness has the nature of an affliction.

Not only is he lazy himself, but he also wishes to influence others to be lazy. He basically doesn't want anybody to do anything at all. "However you people cultivate, I will not cultivate. I will influence you not to cultivate either. I am so lazy that if you are near me for two days, before the third day is up you will be lazy too." He wants other people to follow him in his laziness, so it is called a "following" affliction.

3) The third large subsidiary affliction is *laxity*. People afflicted by laxity don't want to behave properly. Not only do people with this affliction not behave properly themselves, but they also hope that no one else will, either. For example, someone who likes to drink would like to cast everyone into a sea of liquor and pickle them in it. He pitches everyone else into whatever he likes himself. He wants to go dancing, so he drags everyone off to the dance-hall. When he goes to the movies, he takes everyone he knows to the movies. He likes going down to the hells, so he drags everyone down to the hells. He wants to be a hungry ghost, so he says, "There is no one better than a hungry ghost. Come on, come on, right away!" Then he takes all of his friends and relatives off to the path of the hungry ghosts. Or he wants to be an animal and says,

---

[29.] The reference to the response to the ability of Shen-guang (Hui-guo), the Second Patriarch, in lecturing on the sutras before he encountered Bodhidharma.

"I have certainly had enough of being a person. It is best to be a dog. Look at the dog. He doesn't have to work, and on top of that people give him food to eat and take care of him. That's very good. Let's be dogs." Not only does he wish to be a dog himself, but he drags his friends and relatives off on the path to the canine kingdom where they all become dogs together. That is what laxity is about.

4) *Drowsiness*, the fourth large subsidiary affliction, can get into anyone's body. For example, someone is listening to the sutra, or sitting in meditation, and he supposes that he has entered samadhi, but has merely dozed off. "I heard what was said very, very clearly," he insists. "My head just fell over; it wished to draw near to my feet and make friends." That is drowsiness. No matter what you are doing, you don't have any energy, and you just want to go to sleep. You go to sleep, yet still feel that you didn't sleep. Even if you didn't actually go to sleep, you are still none too clear. You listen to someone saying, "Thus I have heard," in an extremely loud voice, yet you do not hear.

5) The fifth large subsidiary affliction is *restless inattention*. What is the meaning of this one? You are sitting upright, listening to a sutra, and then all by itself your head starts to jerk. This is not to say that it is like Ananda's head moving to the left and right in order to look at the light emitted from the Buddha's hands. In this case, since there is no light, you don't know who told your head to move. In fact, you don't wish to move it. The head moving by itself is a case of restless inattention.

Another aspect of restless inattention is the constant affliction in your mind, which you are never quite able to get rid of completely. Since the affliction is constantly being generated, your mind is not at peace. "I don't know what's best. Since listening to this sutra is not at all interesting, maybe I will just sit here and meditate." That is restless inattention; the mind is not tranquil. You always feel like you are sitting on pins and needles, yet it is even more painful than that. Unless I had told you, you wouldn't have known that restless inattention is one of the eight large subsidiary afflictions. If you are afflicted with it often, your mind will find no peace.

Restless inattention could literally be translated as "putting down and picking up." You put something down and then pick it up again; put it down and pick it up again. What should you do about this affliction? You should put it down; you should get rid of it.

6) The sixth of the large subsidiary afflictions is *loss of mindfulness* – literally, loss of thought. "Since it is best not to have false thoughts," you say, "how can this be called an affliction?" What is meant is loss of proper thought. For example, you wish to recite the Buddha's name, so you recite three times: "Namo Amita Buddha, Namo Amita Buddha, Namo Amita Buddha," and then you forget; you no longer remember the thought of it. You wish to recite the Shurangama Mantra:

> *The wonderfully deep dharani,*
>   *the unmoving Honored One.*
> *The Foremost Shurangama King*
>   *is seldom found in the world.*
> *It melts away my deluded thoughts*
>   *gathered in a million kalpas...*

"Huh, what comes next?" It is like when you are all reciting a sutra or mantra and everyone stops in the middle, not knowing what point you have recited to. That is the loss of mindfulness; your thought which recites the mantra has been lost. It is certainly not the case that none of you are reciting or making any noise because you have all entered the no-sound samadhi. No. It is just that you have lost your mindfulness.

7) The seventh large subsidiary affliction is *improper knowledge*, in other words, deviant knowledge and views instead of right knowledge and views. A person with improper knowledge says that right is wrong and wrong is right, white is black and black is white, good is bad and bad is good. For instance, I heard some people saying, "Eating a lot is an ascetic practice." That is a case of

deviant knowledge and views. Because they say that eating a lot is called a most difficult ascetic practice, they all eat as if their lives were at stake. To call that an ascetic practice is nothing but improper knowledge.

8) The eighth of the large subsidiary afflictions is *distraction*, lack of samadhi-power. This is the mirror illuminating outwardly. It is like a camera, which can only take photographs of people outside of the camera; it cannot photograph its own inside. Distraction comes from the lack of samadhi, and it is cured by the practice of dhyana samadhi.

There are still six basic afflictions, with which I believe you are all very familiar. You could say that they are old friends.

1) The first is *greed*. Your greed, my greed, and others' greed are all alike – three in one and one in three. People are not the same, but their greed is all alike. Their greed differs, however, in amount. You have a little more greed and I have a little less, or you have a little less greed and I have a little more. Every person has his own amount.

Greed harms us, but you still are not aware of it. Why haven't you realized Buddhahood yet? Why are you so stupid and lacking in wisdom? Do you understand now? It is just because of greed. Greed is insatiable; it has no fear of an excess of anything, whether it be money, or things, or garbage. Greed isn't afraid of a lot of afflictions, either. The more the better. And so it was said of Han Hsin, the great general of the Han Dynasty, "When Han Hsin made use of troops, it was 'the more the better.'" "The more the better" is a manifestation of greed, the first of the basic afflictions.

2) The second is *anger*. Anger is your ignorance; it is the very fiery energy of your firecracker-like temper. I say it is like a firecracker, but because atomic and hydrogen bombs have now been developed, the ignorance and anger in the minds of people today are as tremendous and fierce as the awesome power of the atomic and hydrogen bombs.

3) The third basic affliction is *stupidity*. Why do we always do things wrong? It is our stupidity which causes us to do things which we shouldn't do. What we shouldn't learn we want to learn. For instance, now many young people take drugs which cloud the mind. These drugs certainly should not be taken, yet they take one pill and want to take another pill, and still want to take one pill more. They think about it, but they don't actually know why they want to take more. The reason is that they are stupid. They suppose that there will be another world inside the cave.[30] They suppose that in taking a certain pill, there will be a new discovery, one as momentous as Columbus' discovery of a new continent. They want to discover a new continent by taking drugs. Wouldn't you say that is stupid? Their stupidity turns them upside down.

4) The fourth basic affliction is *pride*, or arrogance.

5) The fifth is *doubt*. Doubt is a lack of faith, a lack of belief. When doubt arises, one doubts everything. One doubts the gods, doubts the ghosts, doubts right and doubts wrong, doubts oneself and doubts others, doubts right principles and doubts what is unprincipled also.

6) The sixth is *deviant views*. The knowledge and views held by someone with this affliction are most improper.

Now that I have finished explaining the afflictions, I hope that everyone's afflictions have been ended. You shouldn't think that the afflictions are your friends and relatives. You should abandon them and stop helping them create the karma of offenses. If you help the afflictions, they will help you create karmic offenses which will fall back on you. Afflictions are the *mahasattvas*, the great beings, who pay no attention to others[31]; they won't pay any attention to whether or not you are punished or to whether or not your retribution is summoning you. When you undergo

---

[30.] The allusion is to Chinese beliefs concerning the existence of other worlds which can be entered through certain caves in the sacred mountains and elsewhere. A well-known example of this theme is in Tao Yuan-ming's celebrated work "The Peach-Blossom Spring" (*Tao-hua Yuan Qi*).

punishment, then the afflictions flee far away and disappear. When you go to the hells, why are there no more afflictions to follow along with you to produce more affliction? That is the time the afflictions leave.

All the six basic afflictions and the twenty subsidiary afflictions are included in the second of the Four Truths, **accumulating**. Because the truth of accumulating beckons so many afflictions, the turning by manifestation is, "This is accumulating; its nature is feelings which beckon." What do the feelings beckon? They beckon the afflictions, and it is your afflictions that keep you from attaining genuine wisdom. Should you wish to attain genuine wisdom, you must first defeat the afflictions. In order to defeat them, you must first recognize that they are afflictions. If you don't, what will you defeat? If you have no idea at all what afflictions are, how will you be victorious? It is like wanting to kill thieves. They too are people. As it says in the *Shurangama Sutra*[32], you must know where the thieves are and must recognize what they look like; otherwise, when you are face to face with them, you will take them to be good friends instead of the very people who were the ones who stole your things and who will rob you of all your treasures. Our afflictions are just the same way. If you recognize situations of affliction for what they are, then you will no longer be affected by them, and you can defeat them.

We are continuing the discussion of the dharma of the Four Truths: suffering, accumulating, extinction, and the Way. I have already spoken about the three kinds of suffering, the eight kinds of suffering, and all the infinite kinds of suffering. I have also spoken about the truth of accumulating, that is, about the six basic

---

[31.] The allusion is to the ironic Buddhist ditty:

Mahasattva – don't pay attention to others;
Amita Buddha – everyone for himself.

[32.] "It is just like when a king dispatches troops against bandits who have invaded his country. The troops must know where the bandits are in order to chase them off."

afflictions and the twenty subsidiary afflictions which form part of the truth of accumulating.

The third of the Four Truths, **extinction**, is explained as meaning both "unmoving" and "such, such." When you have been certified as having attained the truth of extinction, you have attained genuine happiness. The four attainments of Nirvana are permanence, bliss, self, and purity. This attainment is the receipt of certification of the fruition called "still extinction." However, it is still the fruition of the small vehicle, not the ultimate and wonderful fruition of the great vehicle. It is a partial principle of truth to which Arhats are certified as having attained. They cut off the birth and death of the delimited segment – the body – but have not yet attained final liberation from the birth and death of the fluctuations. By ending the birth and death of the delimited segment, those of the two vehicles, Arhats and Pratyekabuddhas, attain the bliss of still extinction and destroy the delusions of views and thought.[33]

Deluded views refer to the arising of craving for what you see. The craving which arises in your mind as a result of confronting a certain situation is called a view-delusion; you are confused by the situation.

Thought-delusion, on the other hand, refers to confusion about the principles of the Way. Because you don't understand them, your mind gives rise to the making of distinctions. When distinctions are made, the more you make, the farther away you get. The farther away you get, the more distinctions you make. This "taking the wrong road" is called thought-delusion. When you are certified as having attained the bliss of still extinction, you cut off the delusions of both thought and views. Yet you are still able only to make ignorance surrender; you have not yet eradicated it. Not only in the state of an Arhat, but in all states of enlightenment up to and including the state of the Equal-Enlightenment Bodhisattva, there still exists a very last portion of ignorance characterized by production which has not been destroyed. Therefore, even when one is certified as having attained the fruition which is still extinction, ignorance still exists; however, it does not appear.

Although the birth and death of the delimited segment has already been ended, the birth and death of the fluctuations still exists.

What is meant by the birth and death of the fluctuations which continue even after the attainment of still extinction? The fluctuations refer to the thoughts we give rise to: one thought after another, the first then the next then the one after, thought after thought, unceasingly. The unending transformation of the flow of thought is called the birth and death of the fluctuations. The

---

[33.] There are eighty-eight delusions of view, which are cut off suddenly, and eighty-one delusions of thought, which are gradually eliminated.

There are ten basic delusions of view which manifest themselves in relation to the Four Truths in each of the three worlds – desire, form, and formless. The ten are greed, hatred, stupidity, arrogance, doubt, the view of (bodily) self, one-sided views, deviant views, the view of being attached to views, and the view of grasping (non-beneficial) prohibitive precepts.

In the desire realm, all ten operate in relationship to the truth of suffering, while seven (all except the view of self, one-sided views, and the view of grasping prohibitive precepts) operate in relation to the truths of accumulating and extinction, and eight (all except the view of self and one-sided views) operate in relation to the truth of the Way. In the form and formless realms the relationships of the delusions to the Truths follows the same order with the exception of hatred in relation to all four Truths, since hatred must be eliminated before one can enter samadhi. Thirty-two delusions of view in the desire realm, twenty-eight in the form realm, and twenty-eight in the formless realm total eighty-eight.

There are nine degrees of delusions of thought, which manifest themselves on nine separate grounds. The nine degrees are simply the higher superior, the higher intermediate, and the higher inferior; the middle superior, the middle intermediate, and the middle inferior; the lower superior, the lower intermediate, and the lower inferior. The nine grounds are the five destinies (*gati*).

Upon cutting off the eighty-eight delusions of view one becomes a first-stage Arhat (*srotaapanna*, "Stream-winner"). Upon eliminating the first six degrees of the first ground, one becomes a second-stage Arhat (*sakrdagamin*, "Once-Returner"). Upon eliminating the final three degrees of the first ground, one becomes a third stage Arhat (*anagamin*, "Never-Returner"). When all the remaining 72 are eliminated, one becomes a fourth-stage Arhat (*arhat*). Sometimes only the fourth stage is referred to as Arhatship.

production of one thought is a birth, and the extinction of one thought is a death.

Why is it called birth and death? It is because genuine samadhi has not been attained. When one enters samadhi, coarse thoughts and desires stop. When the first dhyana, called the ground of bliss born of separation, is attained, the pulse stops. When you reach the second dhyana, called the ground of bliss born of samadhi, your breath stops. At the third dhyana, called the ground of wonderful happiness apart from bliss, your thought stops. In the fourth dhyana, called the ground of clear purity which discards thought, there are no fine thoughts. However, attainment of the four dhyanas is not a verification of the fruition of enlightenment. They are nothing more than temporary realizations which come as a result of cultivating the Way. Moreover, the four dhyanas are not very high levels. Most ordinary people who cultivate the Way can probably attain the fourth dhyana.

"This is the Way; you should cultivate it." In discussing the question of the **Way**, I will first explain the Chinese character *dao* 道, "Way." The character contains an element indicating "going" or "walking" 辶. This tells you to practice; only then is the Way of use. Because you need to cultivate according to the Way, it is said, "The Way is to be practiced; if you don't practice it, of what use is the Way?" If you don't cultivate, then the Way is the Way and you are you; the two cannot be united into one. If you cultivate according to Dharma, that is, if you practice the Way, then the Way is you and you are the Way. The Way and you are fundamentally inseparable. It is said of the virtuous nature, "Virtue is to be practiced; if it is not practiced, how can there be virtue?" That is not to say, "Day in and day out I say, 'Act virtuously, act virtuously, act virtuously.'" You practice virtue with your mouth, but you don't actually practice any virtue at all. Not only do you not practice virtue, but you create bad karma with your body. In that case there is no virtue at all. Thus the saying, "Hanging out a sheep's head and selling dog-meat." If you talk about acting virtuously, then you must do it.

Above the element which designates "going" 辶 in the character *dao*, the character *shou* 首 is added. *Shou* is defined as that which is "ahead" or "foremost." In other words, cultivation is the most important business in the whole world. If you wish to end birth and death, then you must cultivate the Way. If you don't wish to end birth and death, you need not cultivate the Way. To end birth and death is certainly not to be afraid of birth and death. Someone who is afraid of birth and death really likes being alive, but he is extremely afraid when he is dying. That is to be afraid of birth and death. If you wish to end birth and death, cultivation of the Way must be foremost; therefore, the character *shou*, foremost, is part of the character *dao*, the Way. If you don't cultivate the Way, then you cannot end birth and death.

We will now divide the character *shou* 首 further. There are two dots ⸜ on top, then a line 一, and below them the character *zi* 自, which means "self." In cultivation, it is you yourself who must cultivate. It isn't that you tell other people to cultivate: "You should cultivate; you should end birth and death; you should act virtuously." That isn't what is meant. You must cultivate the Way yourself. The one important matter is for you to do it yourself, so there is the character, *zi*, in the character meaning Way. Do it yourself!

The horizontal line above the *zi* is the character *yi* 一, "one." What should you do? Find the one. Of what use is it? From the one, everything in the world is generated. One is the beginning. Only after one are there two, then three, then four, then five, up to an infinite number. They are all generated from the number one. The infinite is generated from the one. The infinite is itself the one. If there is no one, then there is no infinite. If there is no infinite, then there is no one. I don't believe that anyone at all has a way to oppose the principle which I am explaining. Anyone who understands mathematics knows that mathematics begins from one. The one is the infinite, and the infinite is the one.

We want neither one nor infinity. There is no one and there is no infinity. No infinity and no one. They change into nothing at all, which is zero. The **0** contains all existence. True emptiness is in the **0**, and wonderful existence is in it too. Where does the **0** come from? It is a shape made by changing the one. You make a circle and that is a **0**; you open it up and it turns into a one. Therefore, the **0** is the original substance of the one. Not only is the **0** the original substance of the one, it is also the original substance of everything between heaven and earth. And it is also the great bright storehouse, the nature of the Treasury of the Thus Come One, that is, the Buddha nature. The Buddha nature is the **0**.

One evening when I was walking down the road with a disciple, there was a little boy who asked his mother, "What has no beginning and no end?" The mother said, "I don't know," and the little boy replied, "A circle." I asked him, "Why do you have the thought of a circle?" The child didn't answer. The **0** represents the nature of the Treasury of the Thus Come One and everything which is generated and changes in the world: true emptiness and wonderful existence, wonderful existence and true emptiness. The **0** has no beginning and no end. If you want to destroy the **0**, cut it and it will turn into a one. What is the one? Ignorance. The change into the one is the change into ignorance. When there is no one, the circle which has not been destroyed is the nature of the Treasury of the Thus Come One. When the circle is destroyed, it turns into ignorance. One is the beginning of ignorance. Didn't I just say that the infinite is made from the one and the one is made from the infinite?

One little bit of affliction produces infinite afflictions. Infinite afflictions are generated from a single small bit of affliction. Why do you do so many mixed-up things? It is because of the one small bit of ignorance. All your confused deeds, so much confused activity, so much karma, so much affliction are produced from the one. Therefore, if you want to cultivate the Way, you must return the one to its original source and turn it into a **0**. Only when you turn it into a **0** can you return to the original source, to the nature which is the Treasury of the Thus Come One, to true emptiness and to wonderful existence. That is what the one is about.

The two dots ⌄ on the top of the character *dao* 道 are one *yin* and one *yang*. The *I Ching*, the *Book of Changes*, says, "One *yin* and one *yang* are the Way." "One-sided *yin* and one-sided *yang* are sickness."[34] Perhaps there is pure *yin* which changes into a ghost or pure *yang* which changes into a god. Therefore, it is said, "One-sided *yin* and one-sided *yang* are sickness." They are divided. The character *yi*, "one," is divided to produce the two dots. Ignorance generates view-delusion and thought-delusion, so the two dots can also be said to be view-delusion and thought-delusion. I have just talked about cutting them off. The two dots, representing view-delusion and thought-delusion, get together to produce countless, numberless delusions. And all of them are generated from the one.

If you wish to return to the original source, turn the one into a **0** again. How? It's not very difficult. You need only work hard every day in cultivating the Way, in sitting in meditation and looking into dhyana, and then you can return to the origin; you can change into a **0**, into the great bright treasury which is your original nature.

Because you say, "I don't believe it," you are still in darkness. If you do believe it, then you can return to your great bright treasury. Because you don't believe in this dharma-door, day in and day out ignorance and affliction never leave you, and you change into what in the Chan School is called a "barrel of black energy." If you believe in this dharma-door, then you can return to your originally existent wisdom, return to the source, and attain to the great bright treasury. You can return to your own great, perfect mirror wisdom, to the wisdom whose nature is equality, to the wonderful investigative wisdom, and to the wisdom of successful performance.

I have just explained only a very little bit about the character *dao* – not even one ten-millionth. Were I to talk about it in detail, I am afraid that it would take a very long time, and I would not be able to finish. Why? Because it is so wonderful. The Great Master

---

[34.] The general idea is that sickness is the result when the *yin* and *yang* of the body are not in balance.

Chih-i, the Wise One, spoke for ninety days about the word "wonderful" (*miao* 妙). If you were to speak clearly about the character *dao*, I'm afraid you couldn't finish talking about it in ninety years, not just ninety days. I am afraid that my lifespan in this lifetime will not be that long, so I can only say a little bit.

Nevertheless, I will still say a little bit more about the character *dao*. The two dots, the one *yin* and one *yang*, can be written to form the character 人 (*ren*, "person"). The Way is not in the heavens, nor is it in the hells, nor is it among animals or hungry ghosts. It is among people. Every person can cultivate the Way; every person can realize the Way; every person possesses the Way from the beginning. It is not obtained from outside. Your successful cultivation of the Way is simply the realization of the Way of the Buddha. Since you haven't yet cultivated the Way to realization, has your Way been lost? No, every person is a fulfillment of the Way.

If you are talking about the heavens, you can say that the sun and the moon are in the two dots. One dot is the sun, and one is the moon. Speaking of people, you can say that the two dots are the two eyes. Ultimately, it is necessary to use your wisdom-eye to cultivate the Way, it is necessary to have wisdom to return the one to the origin and change it into a **0**. **0** is the nature of the Treasury of the Thus Come One; it is a great, bright treasury. It is the Buddha-nature you and I fulfill together. If you are able to return to that Buddha-nature, then in this very body you will immediately realize Buddhahood and will not have to wait to cultivate blessings and wisdom for three asamkhyeya kalpas and to develop hallmarks and minor characteristics for a hundred kalpas. You won't have to wait for such a long time, but can realize Buddhahood immediately. Why haven't you realized it? Because you don't know the Way; you haven't cultivated the Way; there was no one who taught you the Way. Therefore, until now you have been born and died, died and been reborn, birth and death, death then birth. Your turning back and forth in the revolving wheel of the six paths can also be said to be jumping into the **0**.

Into what **0** do you jump? Into the **0** of the revolving of the six paths, which turns you back and forth. Suddenly you are in the heavens; suddenly you are back on earth; suddenly you are a hungry ghost; suddenly you are an animal; suddenly you are a god; suddenly you are in the hells; suddenly you are an *asura*; suddenly you are a person again. You revolve back and forth inside it, unable to jump out in order to keep from spinning around. If you can jump out, destroy the one, and return to the **0**-rigin, then you will have returned to the great Treasury of the Thus Come One, which is your original ground, your originally existent homeland.

Each of the sufferings exerts pressure, and all attack together. This line of verse and the following one have already been explained. "Each of the sufferings" refers to the three kinds of suffering, the eight kinds of suffering, and all the infinite kinds of suffering. Each comes to oppress people, and they all attack together.

Accumulating is feelings which beckon, each unlike the other. Whatever affliction you have beckons more of that affliction. Thus they accumulate.

Only through extinction can the ultimate joy be attained. Only through extinction can the ultimate happiness of Nirvana be attained.

Therefore this is the Way that should be practiced to awaken to the emptiness of dharmas. Everyone should cultivate this Way and awaken to the emptiness of both people and dharmas. You should not be attached. Therefore, the sutra says, **no suffering, no accumulating, no extinction, no Way**. All must be emptied.

Through three turnings of the Four Truths, the Dharma wheel revolves. The three turnings of the Dharma wheel of the Four Truths have already been explained.

Seven shares in enlightenment, the eightfold upright Path, intention, mindfulness, and diligence. The thirty-seven categories of the Way are comprised of seven divisions: the seven shares in enlightenment (sometimes called the seven shares in Bodhi), the eightfold upright Path, the five faculties, the five powers, the four bases of psychic power, the four dwellings in mindfulness, and the four types of upright diligence.

The seven shares in enlightenment are:

1) Choosing a dharma;
2) Vigor;
3) Joy;
4) Rejecting;
5) Giving up;
6) Mindfulness;
7) Samadhi.

Your cultivation should be in accord with these seven dharmas.

Choosing a dharma, the first share in enlightenment, means the choosing of a method. The Chinese word *jiao* 覺, "enlightenment," also means "understanding." You should choose a method for cultivation. You should have the selective dharma-eye which knows right dharma and wrong dharma, good dharma and evil dharma, black dharma and white dharma. When you have the power of selection, you are incapable of taking right as wrong, black as white, and good as bad. Without the share in enlightenment for choosing a dharma, you pick the wrong method.

Once you pick a method, you must cultivate according to it. If you cultivate according to a dharma, then you should have *vigor*, the second share in enlightenment. Your vigor should be upright and not deviant. Upright vigor may refer to your sitting in meditation, or to your holding mantras, or studying the teachings, or maintaining the precepts, or cultivating patience – all the kinds of vigor which are a help to you. If you don't have vigor, then today you sit in meditation and tomorrow you don't; one day you maintain the precepts and the next day you don't; today you cultivate patience and tomorrow you don't. That is to lack the vigor share in enlightenment. If you have the vigor share in enlightenment, in the six periods of time, that is, in the three periods of the day and in the three periods of the night, you are constantly vigorous and never at rest.

Once you have vigor, you can obtain the dhyana bliss that is the share of enlightenment called *joy*. For instance, when you sit in meditation and develop a little spiritual skill, a little *gong fu*, you feel happier than you would be doing anything else. The attainment of that kind of happiness is the share of enlightenment called joy, a kind of clear, tranquil, and especially happy state which is attained in dhyana meditation.

Some experiences in meditation are real, but sometimes it is easy to "let the fire go so the demons can enter" – to become possessed and go crazy. That can happen when you get into a frame of mind in which you chase after experiences and get attached to them. You think to yourself, "Oh, what was that experience like?" To always be thinking about how good it was is simply to be attached to it. Since you are attached, it is easy to become possessed and go crazy. The demon king comes to disturb you. If you don't have any attachments, the demon king can't do anything. If you are attached, then the demon king is in a good position. He makes appear whatever situation you are attached to. In response you should make use of the share of enlightenment for vigor and also the share of enlightenment for rejecting.

Rejecting, the fourth share in enlightenment, means to look deeply into every evil, illuminating and contemplating what is not right, and rejecting it, while, of course, keeping and protecting what is right.

What is not right is whatever you are attached to. You should get rid of attachment, too. Letting attachment go is the share of enlightenment called *giving up*. Letting go teaches you to give up both your false thinking and your attachments. If you don't give them up, you won't be able to attain samadhi and will not obtain the share of enlightenment called giving up.

If you give up your attachment of false thinking, you will be able to guard a vigorous *mindfulness* in every thought. This is the vigor mentioned above. You should never forget it, and in thought after thought you should be mindful of the here and now. And if you cultivate vigorously that way, you will attain the *samadhi* share of enlightenment.

The *Eightfold Upright Path* consists of the following:

1) *Upright views.* "Views" refers to your opinions. They have not yet become external; upright views are held in the mind. The meaning is that you should have a proper viewpoint. If your views are not upright, then it is easy to take a deviant road. If they are upright, then you take the right road. Which views are upright and which are deviant? An upright view would be: "I should study the Buddhadharma, because the Buddhadharma is upright." What is a deviant view? For instance, you gamble or do whatever is enjoyable and leisurely, you are lazy or you harm people – these are all activities born of your deviant views. Therefore, upright views are very important.

2) *Upright consideration.* No sooner do your proper opinions come into being then you think, "Is it right or wrong?" An upright consideration would be: "I think that studying the Buddhadharma is the most genuine business of humanity, and there is nothing wrong with it."

Perhaps you have deviant considerations: "I am afraid that this business of studying the Buddhadharma isn't of any use. Now it is the scientific age. The Buddhadharma talks this way and that about teaching people to do good deeds and to be good people. Nowadays, who is a good person? There aren't any. What everybody does is evil. I see that people commit all sorts of evil deeds, but at the same time these people have money to spend and liquor to drink." Since they have everything, they think that studying the Buddhadharma is not that good, so they run off down a deviant road. If your consideration is upright, you won't.

3) *Upright speech.* If you have upright thought, you are capable of upright speech. What you say doesn't induce people to take deviant paths; it isn't drunken or mad, but always very precise

and correct. You make everybody listen and like to listen and like acting in accordance with what you say.

4) *Upright occupation.* Upright speech leads you to an upright occupation, which is to say, one which most people think is wholesome and not one which is against the law.

5) *Upright living.* If your occupation is upright, then your lifestyle will be upright also.

6) *Upright vigor.* You should be vigorous in doing what is upright, not in doing what is improper.

7) *Upright mindfulness.*

8) *Upright samadhi.*

The *Four Bases of Psychic Power* are:

1) The *desire-basis.* This desire is wholesome, a hoping for good things.

2) The *vigor-basis.*

3) The *mind-basis.*

4) The *volitional basis.*

The *Four Dwellings in Mindfulness* concern body, feeling, mind, and dharmas:

1) Contemplate the body as impure.

2) Contemplate feeling as suffering.

3) Contemplate the mind as impermanent.

4) Contemplate dharmas as having no self.

The *Four Types of Upright Diligence* are:

1) Good roots which have not yet been grown are caused to grow.

2) Good roots already growing are caused to grow further.

3) Evil which has not yet been done is kept from being done.

4) Evil thoughts which have already been generated are cut off.

The *Five Faculties* are:

1) The faculty of faith.
2) The faculty of vigor.
3) The faculty of mindfulness.
4) The faculty of samadhi.
5) The faculty of wisdom.

The *Five Powers* are:

1) Faith has the power of faith.
2) Vigor has the power of vigor.
3) Mindfulness has the power of mindfulness.
4) Samadhi has the power of samadhi.
5) Wisdom has the power of wisdom.

Together the five faculties, the five powers, the four types of upright diligence, the four dwellings in mindfulness, the four bases of psychic power, the seven shares in enlightenment, and the eightfold upright paths make the thirty-seven categories of the Way.

One day connect right through and ripen the fruit of sagehood. If you cultivate the thirty-seven categories of the Way, then one day you will "suddenly connect right through" and be certified as having attained the fruition of sagehood.

Partial truth with residue is just a conjured city. You shouldn't dwell in the kind of nirvana which is a one-sided truth and has residue. That nirvana is a city which has been conjured up; it is not a genuine city. When your attainment of that kind of non-ultimate nirvana has been certified, you must still go forward and cultivate.

No Understanding and No Attaining

Sutra:

And no understanding and no attaining.

Verse:

The Storehouse-Teaching Bodhisattva:
six phenomenal paramitas.
The Perfect cultivates to the point
of wonderful enlightenment,
where noumenon is suddenly clarified.
Without any wisdom, he destroys attachment
and empties every characteristic;
Without attainment, he has no verification
and comprehends the fusion of dharmas.
He makes a jeweled realm appear
on the tip of a single hair.
And he turns the Dharma wheel
while sitting on a speck of dust.
These words are spoken, yet few have faith;
I do not know how many know my sound.

Commentary:

Understanding means wisdom. **Attaining** refers to certification to the attainment of a particular fruition of enlightenment.

When you reach this state, you do not want wisdom, and you do not have a fruition which is verified. There isn't any hope at all. Most people who study the Buddhadharma suppose that they should first study wisdom, and that only after they have learned to be wise will they realize the fruition of Buddhahood. This sutra says that the wisdom of prajna does not exist. There isn't any attainment either. All is empty. It isn't that there isn't any wisdom or attainment; but there isn't any attachment to wisdom, and there isn't any attachment to the place one has attained.

The Bodhisattvas of the Storehouse or Tripitaka Teaching practice the dharma-doors of having wisdom and having attainment. These dharma-doors are called the phenomenal paramitas. Thus the verse says, *The Storehouse-Teaching Bodhisattva: six phenomenal paramitas.*

There are six phenomenal paramitas and six noumenal paramitas. The six noumenal paramitas have no phenomenal characteristics and are without attachment to anything. On the other hand, the six phenomenal paramitas entail attachments. To what? There is attachment to living beings who can be saved and to the Way of the Buddha, which can be realized. To be attached to living beings who can be saved is to have wisdom. To be attached to the Buddha-fruition which can be realized is to have attainment. Now the sutra says, **and no understanding and no attaining**, which indicates that there is no longer an attachment to the six phenomenal paramitas.

The six phenomenal paramitas are:

1) *Giving*, which crosses you beyond miserliness and greed. If you cultivate the paramita of giving, you will not be miserly and greedy. If you are miserly and greedy, you will not give. As soon as you give, you cross beyond the mind of miserly greed.

2) *Maintaining the precepts*, which crosses you beyond defilement and damaging transgressions. When you cultivate and maintain the precepts, you become extremely pure and clear, like a bright pearl. To maintain the precepts is to be without defilement.

If you do not maintain the precepts, you will become dark and dirty from your defilements. Maintaining precepts crosses you beyond defilements. If you do not maintain the precepts, you will become a white piece of paper smudged with black ink: the more stain, the blacker. If you maintain the precepts, the white piece of paper retains the original purity.

3) *Patience under insult,* which crosses you beyond anger. If you cultivate patience, you won't have any temper. If you have a temper, then you don't have patience.

4) *Vigor,* which crosses you beyond laziness. You should be vigorous and courageous every day. To the extent that you are vigorous, you won't be lazy.

5) *Dhyana samadhi,* which crosses you beyond distraction. If you wish to cultivate dhyana samadhi, you must first sit for a long time until you acquire the ability to enter samadhi. When you have entered samadhi, you will no longer be distracted; you will have samadhi-power.

6) *Prajna,* which crosses you beyond stupidity.

The Chinese character *du* 度, "to cross beyond" or "to take across," that is, to save, is used to translate "paramita," but the crossing beyond refers to the six phenomenal paramitas, not to the noumenal ones. The six phenomenal paramitas have perceptible characteristics which can be ascertained in one's behavior. For instance, though you are generous and not miserly, you are still attached to the thought, "Oh, I can give and am not miserly." If you practiced the six noumenal paramitas, your giving would be the same as your not having given. You shouldn't be attached.

The six noumenal paramitas are characterized by there being no attachment anywhere. There are many different levels of the six paramitas; for instance, the non-doing of the six paramitas, which is cultivated by the perfectly enlightened. Basically there is no attachment whatever to what is done; it is equivalent to not having done anything. You say, "When I haven't done something, then, can I say that I have done it? If you can say that my giving is like non-giving, then can we say that non-giving is like giving?" If you give, it is all right to think that it is like not having given, but you cannot say that your not having given is equivalent to your having given.

The Perfect cultivates to the point of wonderful enlightenment, where noumenon is suddenly clarified. The Bodhisattvas of the Perfect Teaching, who are just the same as the wonderful enlightenment Bodhisattvas, cultivate the six noumenal paramitas, along with the Bodhisattvas of the special teaching. They completely understand that giving is the same as not giving and that crossing beyond is the same as not crossing beyond. Therefore, the sutra says, **and no understanding and no attaining**.

Attachment to the six phenomenal paramitas fundamentally does not exist, so the verse says, *Without any wisdom, he destroys attachment and empties every characteristic.* There had been an attachment to prajna, but now all characteristics have been emptied. Therefore, the sutra says, **and no understanding and no attaining**.

Without attaining, he has no verification and comprehends the fusion of all dharmas. There is no attainment to be reached, and there is no attachment to the verification of the fruition of Buddhahood. In other words,

> *Above, there is no Buddha Way*
> *which can be realized.*
> *Below, there are no living beings*
> *who can be taken across.*

That is not to say that there aren't any living beings to take across. But, although they are taken across, they are not taken across. "Although all living beings have been taken across to extinction, there is not a single living being who has been taken across to extinction." It isn't that there aren't living beings to be taken across, but that there is no attachment. There is no understanding or attaining. This enlightenment is the great, perfect mirror wisdom, in which there is no attachment at all. Thus the verse says, he "comprehends the fusion of dharmas."

He makes a jeweled realm appear on the tip of a single hair. When there has been certification to the attainment of such a state, the King's jeweled realm can appear on the tip of a single hair. That is the great manifesting within the small.

And he turns the Dharma wheel while sitting on a speck of dust. This is the doctrine of the *Shurangama Sutra.*

These words are spoken, yet few have faith; / I do not know how many know my sound.[35] There are very few people who believe, so I don't know how many people there are who "know the sound," that is who understand these principles. The Venerable High Master Hsu Yun said, "I have gone everywhere within the boundaries of the heavens in search of someone who knows 'me', but I still don't know if anyone knows my sound." Someone who knows "me" is a friend who knows "himself." The one who knows my sound knows the meaning of what I say. If no one knows my sound, then no matter what I say, nobody understands it. People who understand the principle of what has been said are said to know my sound.

You say, "Dharma Master, I understand what you are saying." Then you know my sound. If you say that you don't understand, then you don't know my sound. If you say, "I understand, yet do not understand," then you know my sound, yet do not. Whether my sound is known or not, I shall still recite these verses and talk about their principles. Whoever cultivates according to them knows my sound. Whoever is not in accord with their principles, and does not cultivate, either, does not know my sound. Whether you know my sound or not is simply whether you believe or not. If you believe in the principles I have talked about, you are one who knows my

---

35. The term *zhi yin* 知音, "one who knows my sound," is usually reserved for a very close friend who deeply understands one.

sound. If you don't, then you are not one who knows my sound. What principles am I talking about?

"He makes a jeweled realm appear on the tip of a single hair." On the tip of a tiny hair is manifest a Buddha-country, a country where the Buddha proclaims Dharma to teach and transform living beings. "And he turns the Dharma wheel while sitting on a speck of dust." Seated upon an extremely small speck of dust – how small is it? You turn the great Dharma wheel to teach and transform living beings. In this kind of state, the large appears within the small. If you understand that state, you are one who knows my sound. If you don't understand, then you should study the Buddhadharma. Study until you too can sit on a speck of dust and turn the Dharma wheel. Then you will understand.

The Meaning of Bodhisattva

Sutra:

Because nothing is attained, the Bodhisattva, through reliance on prajna paramita, is unimpeded in his mind.

Verse:

There is no cultivation, verification, or attainment.
What has characteristics and is conditioned
    has a time of demise,
And Bodhisattvas,
    in becoming enlightened to this truth,
Trust to prajna,
    and became even with the other shore.
The mind without impediments
    leaves the retribution-obstacle behind;
A nature totally, truly empty puts an end
    to words and thoughts.
I send these words to those of future worth:
    seek it in yourself;
A head piled on top of a head
    is the height of stupidity.

Commentary:

When the sutra says, **and no understanding and no attaining**, "no understanding" means not having the wisdom-paramita of the six phenomenal paramitas of the Storehouse-Teaching Bodhisattva, while "no attaining" means no attainment of the nirvana with residue of the two vehicles.

Because nothing is attained: no-attainment is this sutra's purpose and intent. The beneficial function of the *Prajna Paramita Sutra* is the eradication of your attachments, so that your mind has no attachment to attainment and no attachment to verification of the fruition. You should verify, yet not verify; not verify, yet verify. What is meant by verifying, yet not verifying? Although you are certified as having attained the fruition, you shouldn't be attached to having attained it. That is genuine attainment of ultimate nirvana. This is why no-attainment is the sutra's purpose and intent.

The Bodhisattva, through reliance on prajna paramita, is unimpeded in his mind. In order to cultivate, he relies on the deep wisdom of the prajna paramita dharma. What is obtained through cultivation is an unimpeded mind. We cannot be at ease because we have impediments. If you have no impediments, you can be at ease. **Is unimpeded** means that the retribution-obstacle has been eradicated through the use of no-attainment. That is the kind of power this sutra has. No-attainment is this sutra's purpose and intent, and eradicating the three obstacles is its beneficial function.

Because nothing is attained, the Bodhisattva, through reliance on prajna paramita, on the dharma-door of profound prajna, brings about the eradication of the retribution-obstacle, which is to say that he is **unimpeded in his mind**.

The three obstacles are the retribution-obstacle, the activity-obstacle, and the affliction-obstacle, as I explained above. If you have impediments, you cannot destroy the retribution-obstacle. To be **unimpeded** is to attain the state where both people and dharmas are empty.

The verse says, *There is no cultivation, verification, or attainment.* At this level there is no cultivation, because you have finished cultivating; there is nothing to verify, because you have already obtained verification. "What there was to be done is already finished, so you undergo no further existence." Everything that you were supposed to do is done. Because the great matter is all completed, the verse says, "no verification or attainment." No cultivation and no verification means that although one is unable to have a place of attainment, there isn't anywhere to attain to. If you were to have a place of attainment, then you would have a place of attachment. Therefore, the verse continues, *What has characteristics and is conditioned has a time of demise.* If you are attached to the characteristics of conditioned dharmas, there will be a time of demise, since you cannot be without a time of demise forever. If you don't want there to be a demise, there must be "no cultivation, verification, or attainment." You will be unimpeded at the point when you have nothing whatever that is attained.

And Bodhisattvas, in becoming enlightened to this truth, / Trust to prajna, and become even with the other shore. What is the meaning of the word "Bodhisattva?" *Bodhi* means "enlightenment," and *sattva* means "sentient being." The Bodhisattva is one who causes all beings to become enlightened. The term "sentient beings" refers to everything with blood and breath – not only people, but all creatures with a span of life. Those without a span of life are called non-sentient beings. To enlighten sentient beings is to cause all sentient beings to attain an enlightenment the same as one has attained oneself. Not only can one recite the *Shurangama Mantra* oneself, but one wants others to be able to recite it also. It isn't to say, "I'm the only one who can recite it. I don't like other people to be able to recite it, because my being the only one shows that I am not the same as other people." It isn't that way. If you achieve some benefit, then you like other people to have it too. "I listen to sutras myself and gain the benefits of listening to sutras. Because I understand the principles of being a person and of studying the Buddhadharma, I also urge all my friends and relatives to come and listen to the Buddhadharma and to study it, so that all obtain equal benefit." That is what is meant by enlightening sentient beings.

There is another way to talk about it. That is, the Bodhisattva is an enlightened one among sentient beings. What is a Bodhisattva basically? He is just a living being with sentience; nonetheless, he is one among living beings who has attained enlightenment. And now he wants to enlighten all sentient beings. That is the meaning of Bodhisattva.

There are Bodhisattvas of the connecting teaching and Bodhisattvas of the special teaching. There is a kind of Bodhisattva for each of the four teachings[36] – the storehouse, the connecting, the special, and the perfect. If the measure of your mind is fairly large, you are a Bodhisattva of the connecting teaching. If the measure of your mind has grown so that you are like Samantabhadra Bodhisattva or Avalokiteshvara Bodhisattva or Earth Store Bodhisattva or Manjushri Bodhisattva, you are a Bodhisattva of the perfect teaching. If you are just a little short of perfect, then you are a Bodhisattva of the special teaching. There are also ten grounds of Bodhisattvahood: there is the Bodhisattva of the first ground, the Bodhisattva of the second ground, the Bodhisattva of the third ground, and so forth to the tenth ground[37]. There are myriad

---

[36.] The four teachings are a classification according to Hua-yan (Xian-shou) School of Buddhism in China.

[37.] The ten grounds are:

1. joy (*pramudita*),
2. apart from defilement (*vimala*).
3. light-emitting (*prabhakari*),
4. brilliance (*arcismati*),
5. difficult to conquer (*sudurjaya*),
6. manifesting (*abhimukhi*),
7. far-reaching (*duramgama*),
8. unmoving (*acala*),
9. wholesome wisdom (*sadhumati*), and
10. Dharma-cloud (*dharmamegha*).

distinctions among the Bodhisattvas, just as there are various classes among people. In short, the Bodhisattva is enlightened to the truth of the Way of no-attachment and to the dharma of the unimpeded mind, and he therefore understands these principles.

Bodhisattva is an extremely spiritual and holy name. Chinese people say *pu sa*, which is a simplified form of address, a shortened form of the Chinese transliteration *pu ti sa tuo*. Some people claim they are Bodhisattvas, although they are not. Some people who are Bodhisattvas will not admit it. You see, it is very strange: those who are not Bodhisattvas say they are, while those who are don't say so. Ultimately, whether you say so or not, those who aren't, aren't, and those who are, are. So there is no need to say so. Bodhisattvas don't advertise themselves in the newspaper saying, "Do you recognize me? I am a Bodhisattva." It isn't like that.

How is it then? A Bodhisattva must have the Bodhisattva mind; he must cultivate the Bodhisattva practices and do what a Bodhisattva does. It isn't a matter of merely saying, "I am a Bodhisattva." If you talk that way, then you are nothing but a demon-obstructed ghost. You are just like those deviant gods outside the Way who through automatic writing impersonate others by saying, "I am *Guan-di Gong*[38]." What are they really? They are just small ghosts, or not even small ghosts; they are merely conjured up by animals with deviant knowledge and views, like the yellow-skinned weasel[39], which impersonates this or that god. Genuine Bodhisattvas don't need to say, "Look at me. I am a Bodhisattva." For example, when the President travels, he doesn't need to introduce himself: "I am the President of the United States. Do you

---

[38.] A hero of the Period of the Three Kingdoms in China (222-265 A.D.), who was said to have become a god after his death. In his role as a Buddhist Dharma-protector he is also known as Bodhisattva Qie-lan.

[39.] *you shu* 鼬鼠. The yellow fur from its large tail is especially prized for making calligraphy brushes for writing tiny characters. If these creatures are able to live for a thousand years, their fur turns black, after ten thousand years, white. After a hundred years they begin to develop a certain amount of psychic power, similar to that of the "fox essence".

know me?" Everyone already knows him. "Here comes Mr. So-and-So, the President of the United States." So it isn't necessary to put advertisements in the paper saying, "I am a Bodhisattva." If you are a Bodhisattva or if you aren't, people will recognize you for what you are.

What proof do Bodhisattvas have? I'll tell you. Bodhisattvas have ended the two kinds of birth and death. The birth and death of the delimited segment does not exist, and the birth and death of the fluctuations has also been ended. The birth and death of the fluctuations is simply thought: a thought is produced and a thought is destroyed. In samadhi, the thoughts are not produced and destroyed, and so it is said, "The Naga[40] is eternally in samadhi," which means that the birth and death of the delimited segment and of the fluctuations have been ended. That is to be a real, actual, genuine Bodhisattva. But you don't recognize him. The wonderful is right here. You cannot recognize a true Bodhisattva. If you recognize a true Bodhisattva, you are a Bodhisattva too.

"Trust to prajna and become even with the other shore." Relying upon profound prajna, they become even with the other shore, that is, equal to the other shore. Just that is *paramita*, to arrive at the other shore.

The mind without impediments leaves the retribution-obstacle behind. Since your mind has no impediments, you have left the retribution-obstacle behind. What is the retribution-obstacle? Our bodies. Why do we have bodies? Because of impediments. If there are none, "suffering and bliss are a single thusness." There is no birth and no death. Birth is death, and death is birth. In the midst of birth and death, you do not move. In other words, "compliance and opposition are a single thusness." It is that way whether one is going along with situations or going against them.

---

40. *long* 龍, "dragon," but here used as an epithet for the Buddha.

Complying and opposing are a single thusness;
Birth and death are a single thusness;
Suffering and bliss are a single thusness.

In short, there isn't anything at all which can move or shake the "mind without impediments." The mind is immovable precisely because there are no impediments. You have your hang-ups; someone else has his obstructions. To have no hang-ups is to have no obstructions. To have impediments is to be hung up right here where you are. In the midst of impediments, you are not hung up anywhere. Since there fundamentally are no hang-ups, how can there be any impediments? Therefore it is said, "No hang-ups and no obstructions."

To have no impediments is to end birth and death. Therefore, it is said, "Birth and death are nirvana; affliction is Bodhi." If you encounter adherents of the two vehicles who have not understood this principle, and you tell them that affliction is Bodhi and that birth and death are nirvana, they'll be very frightened and become very nervous and they'll run off, saying, "I never heard that dharma before. How can affliction be Bodhi and birth and death be nirvana? I don't believe it." And not believing, they will want to leave.

The Bodhisattva, on the other hand, is enlightened to affliction being Bodhi and birth and death being nirvana. All you have to do is turn your head and body around, that's it!

Why don't we understand Bodhi? Because we have turned our backs on enlightenment and are together with the defilements. If you can turn your back on the defilements, then you are together with enlightenment. That is to be without impediments. When your mind is unimpeded in the midst of every situation – birth and death, suffering and happiness, compliance and opposition – you remain unmoved. Just that is to be **unimpeded**. Then you are apart from the retribution-obstacle, that is, you are able to leave the impediment of your body.

Why are we unable to leave our bodies? Why do we see our bodies as so important? Everybody seeks fame and fortune. Day in and day out they "scurry about like restless waves." Why? It is all for the sake of their bodies. They think of ways to be very fine slaves for their bodies, to be very fine horses or cows. They don't want to offend their bodies.

Yet your body is so impolite to you. In what way? The better you are to it, the worse it is to you. It is just as King Prasenajit said to the Buddha,

> *"World-Honored One, in the past when I was young, my skin was moist and shining. When I reached the prime of life, my blood and breath were full. But now in my declining years, as I race into old age, my form is withered and worn. My spirits are dull, my hair is white, and my face is in wrinkles, and I haven't much time remaining."*

His hair was white and his face had row after row of wrinkles, like waves on a great sea. He did not have much time left; he would be dead very soon. All that was because of impediments. If you don't have impediments, then you are not attached to the body which comes as karmic retribution, as a retribution-obstacle. Because you have a body, you have retribution-obstacles. If you don't have any impediments, then you don't have a self; and then there are no retribution-obstacles. Therefore, the verse says, "The mind without impediments leaves the retribution-obstacle behind."

A nature totally, truly empty puts an end to words and thoughts. The Buddha nature, your own nature, is the realization of the principle of the true characteristic of emptiness. But since there is nothing to say about your own nature's original substance of true suchness, the verse says, it "puts an end to words and thoughts." There is nothing to say, and there are no thoughts to think.

I send these words to those of future worth: seek it in yourself. I now have some words for all the worthy ones who cultivate in the future: "Seek it in yourself." If you wish to have no-attainment and no impediments, you must seek within yourself, not outside. Don't look outside yourself for the principle of "no cultivation, verification, or attainment." It is to be sought in oneself. You yourself must reverse the light to illuminate inwardly.

A head piled on top of a head is the height of stupidity. If you want to look outside for the Way, you are really stupid. That is like piling a head on top of your head. Isn't that truly stupid? Instead of looking outside, you should reverse the light to illuminate inwardly. Only if you turn your head and body around, will you have attainment.

Sutra:

> **Because there is no impediment, he is not afraid, and he leaves distorted dream-thinking far behind.**

Verse:

> *Having no impediments is the true letting go;*
> *When fear is no more, the activity-obstacles depart.*
> *Distortion left far behind,*
>   *the characteristic of production perishes;*
> *The coarse, fine, and dust-and-sand delusions of*
>   *your dream-thoughts become Thus.*
> *The three obstacles are dissolved,*
>   *the three virtues perfected.*
> *The six faculties are used interchangeably,*
>   *certifying the attainment of the six psychic powers.*
> *When you are capable of this wonderful truth,*
>   *you yourself enjoy its use;*
> *Those who know easily*
>   *enlighten the dark and difficult path.*

Commentary:

If you have no impediments, you will be unafraid. Fearless, you **leave distorted dream-thinking far behind**. Everything that is distorted and all dream-thinking no longer exist. Your lack of fear indicates that you have eradicated your affliction-obstacles.

Having no impediments is not at all easy. For instance, "I don't think about anything at all, except my mother and father." Not bad. That is the way of filial piety; nonetheless, it is also a kind of impediment. Perhaps you say, "I have a friend whom I haven't seen in a long time. Although I think about him constantly, day in and day out, I don't get to see him." That is also an impediment. In short, whatever you don't let go of is an impediment. If you can let go of it, then it isn't one. Therefore the verse says, *Having no impediments is the true letting go.* One isn't attached to anything at all.

I remember that when I was on Ling-yan Mountain in Soochow Province in China, I met a monk who had really let go of everything. He did nothing but cultivate dhyana meditation. He was called Da Xiu. What does it mean to let go of everything? I'll tell you. Da Xiu wrote a verse which said,

> *There is no great or small,*
> *No inside or out.*
> *I cultivate, come to my end,*
> *And make the arrangements all by myself.*

What arrangements did he have to make? In a stone wall he made a hole which was just big enough for one person to sit down in. Then with a slab of rock he made a stone door, which had iron hinges so that it could be opened and closed. Then, all by himself, he sat down inside, closed the door, and came to his end. "I cultivate, come to my end, and make the arrangements all by myself." He sat down inside, closed the door, and perfected the stillness – he entered nirvana. His was the true letting go. He hadn't accepted any disciples, so there weren't a lot of troublesome matters either. That is what is called being **unimpeded**. To have disciples is also to have impediments; having disciples is a lot of trouble. I don't know how much trouble there will be in the future, but I don't pay any attention, because trouble is also not trouble and impediments are also not impediments.

Some people may already have been familiar with the story of Da Xiu, but that does not stop me from talking about him. In explaining sutras, you should not be afraid of talking at length. When you first give sutra lectures, you should speak about what you understand, no matter whether others understand or not. If you don't understand, you should say that you don't understand. When you first practice lecturing on sutras, you should "put your foot down on the actual ground." When you say one sentence, it should be like a hundred pounds of rocks coming down and making a hole in the ground. Anyone who doesn't want to listen has to anyway. "I am going to put this one sentence in your mind, and your mind will have to accept it." So, whether or not people have already heard something, you can always talk about it one more time.

You shouldn't "steal time from work and scrimp on materials" either. For instance, if a house you are building clearly calls for eight-inch beams, and you say, "Oh, it will be all right if I use four-inch beams, since they are a little cheaper," you are scrimping on materials. And perhaps you are supposed to work for eight hours and you only work for six. "I will just create some confusion about those two hours and say that I worked eight." That is to steal time from work. Don't be that way when you lecture on sutras. You must actually do your talking, and not pay attention to whether people understand. You should lecture that way when you are just beginning to lecture, and also in the future. Do you understand? Further, you shouldn't just explain the principles that I tell you to lecture about. Americans talk about the growth of freedom, and so you can let your own freedom develop and express yourself according to your own wisdom. Then there can be new and creative developments.

That is to be like Dharma Master Dao-sheng. Most other people, when they lectured on the *Mahaparinirvana Sutra*, said that *icchantikas* have no Buddha-nature and cannot become Buddhas. But Dharma Master Dao-sheng declared, "Icchantikas[41] have the Buddha-nature too, and they can become Buddhas, right?" Everyone was opposed, but the rocks nodded their heads in agreement. Thus is the meaning of the saying, "Noble Dao-sheng spoke Dharma, and the insensate rocks nodded their heads."[42] Why did they nod their heads? Because he had brought out something new.

You shouldn't just follow my road. If I weren't a genuinely democratic teacher, I wouldn't allow you to develop your own freedom. You certainly would have to follow after me. "If you don't follow me," I'd say, "then your road is confused, you are truly evil, and in the future you will fall into the hells." But I am not like that. I am for the development of freedom. Because I have now come to America, there is the development of freedom. Everyone has his own wisdom, and I can't cover your wisdom up, as if I were putting it in a teacup and not letting it out. Unless you have no wisdom and are incredibly stupid so that you have nothing new to develop, you should be attentive to allowing new developments to come forth. Any disciple may contribute to this, no matter who it is.

When fear is no more, the activity-obstacles depart. Why is there fear? Because there are activity-obstacles – karmic obstacles. When you are no longer afraid, there are no longer any karmic obstacles.

Distortion left far behind, the characteristic of production perishes. We living beings are distorted (*dian dao* 顛倒, literally, "upside down"). If we are able to separate ourselves from the distortion, then the ignorance characterized by production perishes.

The coarse, fine, and dust-and-sand delusions of your dream-thoughts become Thus. If you are without distortion, then you don't have any dream-thoughts. If you are without dream-thoughts, then you don't have any coarse delusions, any fine delusions, or

---

[41.] An *icchantika* is one who has cut off all good roots, and it was considered impossible for such a person to realize Buddhahood.

[42.] The incomplete Fa-xian translation of the *Mahaparinirvana Sutra* (T. 396) states that *icchantikas* could not become Buddhas. Later Dao-sheng (ca. 360-434 A.D.) was vindicated by the arrival of the more complete *Dharmakshema* translation (T. 374), which contained a passage supporting his contention.

any dust-and-sand delusions. Everything has merged with the wonderful truth of true thusness.

The three obstacles are dissolved, the three virtues perfected. At that time your three obstacles, the karmic obstacle, the retribution-obstacle, and the affliction-obstacle, have dissolved. The three virtues which are perfected are the virtue of liberation, the virtue of prajna, and the virtue of the Dharma-body. All three virtues have been fully perfected, perfectly fused.

The six faculties are used interchangeably, certifying the attainment of the six psychic powers. If you are able to use the six faculties interchangeably, then in a wonderful manner each of the faculties has the function of all six. That is to say, you have been able to obtain the six psychic powers. The six faculties are the eye, ear, nose, tongue, body, and mind. In a wonderful manner, each faculty functions in six ways. This is a certification that you have obtained the six psychic powers. At that time, you are able to make use of the power of the heavenly eye, the power of the heavenly ear, the power with regard to past lives, the power with regard to the minds of others, the spiritually based psychic powers, and the power of the extinction of outflows. You have been certified as having obtained them all.

When you are capable of this wonderful truth, you yourself enjoy its use. When you understand this kind of subtle and wonderful truth, you personally experience its benefit.

Those who know easily enlighten the dark and difficult path. When you understand, it is easy to awaken to this truth (*dao li* 道理, literally, "Way-principle"). If you don't understand then you will be mistaken and take the wrong turn; you will choose the wrong road.

Nirvana

Sutra:

Ultimately Nirvana!

All Buddhas of the three periods of time attain annutarasamyaksambodhi through reliance on prajna paramita.

Verse:

Virtue is nowhere incomplete,
and all the obstacles perish;
This final perfect stillness is called nirvana.
Those passed by, not yet come, and now existing,
All Buddhas of the three periods of time,
rooted in a common source,
Through reliance on this prajna paramita,
Reach the genuine and equal enlightenment
of the Supreme Immortal.
If those who practice are capable only
of diligence and vigor,
What worry can there be about not attaining
the field of the Dharma-nature?

Commentary:

Ultimately Nirvana! Because you have destroyed the retribution-obstacle, the karmic obstacle, and the affliction-obstacle, **distorted dream-thinking** can be left **far behind**. If you examine that sentence of the *Heart Sutra*, you will see that all the living beings of the nine dharma-realms are dreaming. The Bodhisattva dreams of seeking the Way of the Buddha above, and of transforming living beings below. He wishes to realize the Way of the Buddha in order to take living beings across, yet it is all in a dream.

The Conditioned-Enlightened, the Pratyekabuddhas, are also dreaming. About what? They dream of looking out for themselves alone. Living deep in the desolate mountain valleys, they are Arhats who "comprehend for their own sakes." That is the meaning of "Looking out for themselves alone, they are incapable of promoting the common good." That is also dreaming.

Hearers, the Shravakas, dream of the one-sided emptiness which is the one-sided truth of nirvana with residue.

The gods have a dream of happiness and peace; they are at ease and enjoy an especially peaceful, superior, and wonderful happiness.

People dream of seeking fame and fortune. They wish to make a lot of money or to become officials. In this life they are all upside down and take suffering to be happiness. Every day they are busy dreaming of fame and fortune.

What dream do the asuras have? They dream of fighting. For instance, it is an asura's situation when someone goes and fights someone else. To be an asura is to be someone who likes to fight, and to be in the dream of fighting.

Those in the hells dream of undergoing bitter suffering. Hungry ghosts dream of starving, and animals dream a dream of stupidity.

Each of the nine dharma-realms has its own dream. The Buddha in ultimate nirvana is the only one who does not dream, and so his is called ultimate nirvana.

People who don't understand the Buddhadharma say, "Nirvana is nothing but dying." Yet that dying is not the same as death, because it is a voluntary dying; it is known and understood. What there was to be done is already done, and pure practice is already established, and so you undergo no further existence. Therefore, you wish to enter nirvana, the state in which there is no birth and death. You yourself know beforehand that you are going to enter nirvana: "At a certain time I will enter nirvana and perfect the stillness." Thus this is dying which is voluntary and understood.

It is said to be understood because when you are about to enter nirvana, you have great clarity. Your body is without sickness or suffering, and your mind has no cravings; it is undistorted. There is no greed in your mind for the objects of the five desires: wealth, sex, fame, food, and sleep. You are not greedy for anything, nor do you long for anything, nor is there any distortion in your mind. When you are about to die, your thoughts are not all distorted and unclear. When people who have cultivated want to enter nirvana, they themselves know it, and they say very clearly to everyone, "in a certain year, a certain month and day, at a certain time, I am going to enter nirvana." Saying it very clearly to everyone is what is meant by "knowing." It is not to say that nirvana is just death; nirvana is no birth and no death. You are only able to die because you were born. If you hadn't been born, you wouldn't die. Therefore, **Ultimately Nirvana**. What is meant by "ultimately nirvana?"

Virtue is nowhere incomplete, and all the obstacles perish. Since there are no obstacles at all, the virtuous nature is fully perfected. The complete lack of obstacles is called perfecting the stillness, and it is also called nirvana.

This final perfect stillness is called nirvana. Perfect stillness is a translation of nirvana. "Perfect" refers to merit which is perfect in every particular; "stillness" refers to virtue which is everywhere still. Virtue is everywhere still because, upon reaching the extreme limit, it merges with the four virtues of nirvana – permanence, bliss, self, and purity – and thus the ultimate happiness called nirvana is attained.

Those passed by, not yet come, and now existing. It is not only Bodhisattvas who cultivate according to this dharma door, but also all the Buddhas of the three periods of time, that is, all the Buddhas of the past, present, and future.

Therefore, the verse says, *All Buddhas of the three periods of time, rooted in a common source.* All the Buddhas of the three periods of time, through reliance upon the profound and wonderful prajna wisdom, are able to attain anuttarasamyaksambodhi, the supreme, the genuine and equal, and the genuine enlightenment. It is supreme in that there is none above it; it is the enlightenment of the Buddha. Genuine and equal enlightenment is the enlightenment of the Bodhisattva. Genuine enlightenment is the enlightenment of those of the two vehicles. The genuinely enlightened are not the same as common people who are unenlightened. Common people do things which are wrong and don't even know that they are wrong. They don't know that they should change. That is to be unenlightened. Genuine enlightenment is the attainment of those of the two vehicles, the Conditioned-Enlightened and the Hearers. Being enlightened, they are not the same as common people, but they have not been able to attain the genuine and equal enlightenment of the Bodhisattva Way, which consists of the six paramitas and ten thousand practices for taking oneself across and for taking others across, for benefitting oneself and for benefitting others. Those of the two vehicles are all Arhats who "comprehend for their own sake." Because they pay attention only to themselves and not to others, they are incapable of genuine and equal enlightenment.

Although Bodhisattvas attain genuine and equal enlightenment, they have not yet attained the supreme enlightenment. The genuine and equal is equivalent to the enlightenment of the Buddha and refers to the Bodhisattvas of equal enlightenment. These Bodhisattvas are different from those of the two vehicles, because the latter comprehend for their own sake, while the Bodhisattva benefits himself in order to benefit others. But the Bodhisattvas of genuine and equal enlightenment are still incapable of the supreme enlightenment.

Only the Buddha is supreme. He is called the Unsurpassed One (*anuttara*) and the Human-Taming Charioteer (*purusadamyasarathi*). His is said to be the supreme, the genuine and equal, and the genuine enlightenment.

The sutra says, **through reliance on prajna paramita**. All the Buddhas of the three periods of time reach the other shore through the use of profound and wonderful prajna wisdom; *through reliance on this paramita*. This verse says, *Reach the genuine and equal enlightenment of the Supreme Immortal*. The Supreme Immortal is the Buddha, who is also referred to as the Greatly Enlightened Golden Immortal.

If those who practice are capable only of diligence and vigor. You people who cultivate need be capable only of going forward and diligently cultivating without retreating. "Don't expose it to the sun for one day and freeze it for ten." Cultivation of the Way is the same: you must cultivate every day. Cultivate every year, cultivate every month, cultivate every day. Cultivate at all times; at all times be vigorous. Every day be vigorous, every month be vigorous, every year be vigorous, in all places and at all times. It is not that I am vigorous today and tomorrow I retreat. It is not to go one step forward and then backward four steps. You shouldn't be like that. That is not vigor.

What worry can there be about not attaining the field of Dharma-nature? If you can be vigorous, you can attain the Dharma-nature, which is represented by a field. Only after you plant things in the field can you have a harvest. You need only be vigorous in plowing and weeding, and then you can harvest. This is the field of the Dharma-nature: you cultivate the Dharma-body yourself, and your own nature will be perfected, and you will realize Buddhahood, which is like harvesting the field of the Dharma-nature. You obtain the fruit.

For instance, there is someone who is so vigorous that he does not even sleep at night but cultivates the Way instead. He cultivates for one night, and then what? He sleeps every day during the day.

That too is the same as not cultivating and cannot be said to be vigor. Vigor is not to say, "All of you sleep; I won't sleep. I'll cultivate the Way." Then you sleep in the daytime when everyone else is awake. That isn't vigor. Not sleeping at night and sleeping during the day amounts to just the same thing.

The Mantra

Sutra:

Therefore, know that prajna paramita is a great spiritual mantra, a great bright mantra, a supreme mantra, an unequalled mantra. It can remove all suffering; it is genuine and not false.

Commentary:

Therefore, know that prajna paramita is a great spiritual mantra. Because of all the various principles discussed above, one knows that the prajna paramita, the wonderful wisdom, a dharma which arrives at the other shore, **is a great spiritual mantra.**

What is the meaning of **great**? This is the great with nothing beyond it; if there were something beyond this great, it would not count as great, but would be small. Since this great has nothing beyond it, there is nothing greater.

What is the meaning of **spiritual**? "Spiritual" is inconceivable. The meaning is just about the same as "wonderful;" nonetheless, "wonderful" (*miao* 妙) has the meaning of "unmoving," while "spiritual" (*shen* 神) has the meaning of "moving;" there is a kind of movement. The wonderful is unmoving, yet moves everything totally and comprehends everything totally. It doesn't function through movement. However, if the spiritual doesn't move, then it is not the spiritual. The spiritual must move. The same word appears in the compound *shen tong* 神通, which means psychic power; the Chinese literally is "spiritual penetration." The "penetration" means a going through; there is movement. But in the wonderful there is knowledge without movement.

The Buddha teaches and transforms living beings in other Buddha-countries to realize the Way and to enter nirvana. He knows everything. The wonderful is right here; without using movement, he knows. But with the spiritual you must go to the place to know about it. The spiritual gets to wherever it is going like a rocket going to the moon. When you arrive on the moon, you know what the moon is made of and you know what the creation of the moon was about. That is to have a little bit of the spiritual. With the wonderful, without having to go there, you still know what the moon is like and what it is all about. It is not necessary to use the powers of science to come to a conclusion about it. You just know. Without moving the Bodhimanda, the Way-Place, you are enlightened about everything and understand everything. With the spiritual, it is necessary to move the Bodhimanda.

Someone with the psychic power of the heavenly eye should go to the space center and tell them beforehand what the moon is like. He should discuss the matter with them and tell them, "I have proof, and if you don't believe me, I will bring back a clump of moon for you to see." *Hard to fathom fully*: that is what the spiritual is like. In the last analysis, it has no perceptible characteristics.

It is **a great spiritual mantra**. What is a **mantra**? Does it tell you to recite it slowly, slowly (*man-man* in Chinese)? No. A mantra is also something inconceivable. It has four meanings:

1) All mantras are the names of god-kings and ghost-kings, like the *pisaca* and *kumbhanda*. You recite the names of god-kings and ghost-kings, and the small gods and ghosts all act reliably. Why? They wonder, "How do you know our ghost-king? How do you know our god-king?" When you recite the mantra, the little gods and ghosts don't dare break the rules.

2) A mantra is like a soldier's password. In the army, there is a different password every day, and only your own people know it. Others don't know it. For example, today it might be "victory". If, for instance, you meet a soldier whom you don't know, you ask him what the password is, he says, "Victory," and you say, "Right." Everyone then knows that he is one of us. If you ask him the password and he says, "Lucky," that's not it, and you know that you will have to start fighting. Why? Because he isn't one of us. Mantras are just like passwords. As soon as the gods and ghosts hear you recite the mantra, they say, "Oh, that's our password," so they all can be depended upon to follow the rules. Otherwise, they would all want to fight.

3) A mantra is a sort of secret language which others don't know. Only a certain person knows. What does he know? For instance, there was once someone who was originally very poor and lowly, so he went abroad where people didn't know him. Since they didn't know who he was, he told them, "I am the king of a certain country, but the generals rebelled and there was a change in government, so I secretly made my escape and came to your country." The king of the country he came to didn't know whether what he said was true or not. Basically he was a phony, but the king supposed that he too was a real king, so he gave him one of the princesses for a wife. Since one of the king's women was given in marriage to the poor and lowly person, he considered himself part of the king's household. Basically he wasn't a king, but he acted like it. Day in and day out he was always losing his temper. Since he couldn't "eat bitter melons," he got angry, and his temper was large. Then someone came who knew him and knew that he was a poor and lowly person. This newcomer said to the woman of the palace who was married to the imposter, "When he gets angry, you need only say these few sentences: 'You were originally a poor and lowly person who drifted in from another country far away. Why must you have such a big temper?' As soon as you say that, he will know, 'Oh, she knows my origins,' and will not get angry any more." The third meaning of "mantra" is just the same. As soon as

you recite the mantra, the gods and ghosts will assume that you understand their origins and that you know what they are all about, and so they don't dare to break the rules where you are concerned.

4) There is another meaning. Mantras are the mind-seals of all Buddhas. They are the secret language of all Buddhas, which can be known only from Buddha to Buddha. Because all other living beings don't know it, mantras are left untranslated. Therefore, it is said, "With one sound the mantra is proclaimed, and living beings perceive it according to their kind." Living beings of every kind understand as soon as they hear the mantra. Although we people don't understand, ghosts understand, gods understand, and animals and asuras all understand it. Therefore, when you recite the mantra, they are all dependable.

It is like the king who wanted something called *saindhava*. Saindhava is a Sanskrit word which has four different meanings: salt, water, chamber-pot, and horse. Saindhava can mean all four. When the king said, "I want saindhava," the officials didn't know whether he wanted salt, water, a chamber-pot, or a horse. When people who were wise heard him, they knew what he wanted according to the situation. For instance, if he wanted saindhava while he was eating, of course he wouldn't have wanted a chamber-pot; he certainly wanted salt. When he was going travelling and wanted saindhava, he certainly wanted a horse. If he was thirsty and wanted saindhava, then he certainly wanted water. And if you saw that he wasn't thirsty, wasn't eating, and wasn't going travelling, then of course, he wanted a chamber-pot. As soon as people with wisdom looked, they knew. A mantra, too, has a lot of meanings; in short, therefore, when you recite it and people with wisdom and gods and ghosts hear it, they understand it and act accordingly.

Verse:

> It is "a great spiritual mantra," hard to fathom fully;
> "A great bright mantra," illuminating a thousand times
>   a thousand times a thousand world systems.
> "A supreme mantra,"
>   the utmost fruition of enlightenment;
> "An unequalled mantra," reaching the ultimate peak.
> All suffering is removed,
>   and the turning wheel comes to rest.
> "Genuine and not false": everyone progresses.
> What has been spoken discloses the profound prajna,
> And briefly explains the dhyana
>   of the Patriarchs of the East and West.

Commentary:

It is "a great spiritual mantra," hard to fathom fully. The meaning of "a great spiritual mantra" has already been discussed. "Hard to fathom fully," means that the mantra is not at all easy to investigate. In other words, you aren't able to imagine what this great spiritual mantra is like. There is no way its inconceivable realm can be known. Both the spiritual, which belongs to movement, and the wonderful, which belongs to stillness, are inconceivable; both movement and stillness are inconceivable. The inconceivability in movement is the spiritual and the inconceivability in stillness is the wonderful. Therefore, the spiritual is the wonderful, and the wonderful is the spiritual. Were it not the spiritual, then it would not be the wonderful, and were it not the wonderful, then it would not be the spiritual. Therefore, the spiritual and the wonderful are "hard to fathom fully." They cannot be known. Because they are too spiritual and wonderful, there is no way to explain them so they will be understood. If they were not the spiritual and the wonderful, then you could talk about them, but you can't talk about the spiritual and wonderful.

"A great bright mantra," illuminating a thousand times a thousand times a thousand world-systems. The *Heart of Prajna Paramita Sutra* is also **a great bright mantra.** It is great brightness, the treasury of light of the Thus Come One; thus the great bright mantra illuminates and destroys all darkness. If you recite the *Heart Sutra*, you illuminate and destroy your darkness, ignorance, and affliction of life after life in limitless previous kalpas. The illumination and destruction of your own affliction and ignorance is done inwardly. When you recite this great mantra, you are also able to emit light outward which illuminates the great trichiliocosm – "a thousand times a thousand times a thousand," or one billion, world-systems. Therefore, the verse says, "'A great bright mantra,' illuminating a thousand times a thousand times a thousand world-systems." The trichiliocosm is the world outside. The afflictions within our very own nature, which can be illuminated and destroyed, constitute the world inside. Inside and out, outside and inside, all is light. Everywhere, inside and out, the bright light which is the original substance of your wisdom manifesting is itself the *Heart of Prajna Paramita Sutra*; it is your very own original wisdom illuminating a billion world-systems.

"A supreme mantra," the utmost fruition of enlightenment. The mantra is said to be supreme because there is none higher, and because it reaches the fruition of Buddhahood. When you recite the *Heart of Prajna Paramita Sutra*, you go step by step by step from the ground of the common person to the ground of Buddhahood, the fruition of enlightenment.

"An unequalled mantra," reaching the ultimate peak. Originally the enlightenment of those of the two vehicles is known as equal enlightenment. "Unequalled" means that nothing can be its equal. In other words, the mantra reaches the very final and ultimate enlightenment, the highest peak of the mountain, "the ultimate peak."

All suffering is removed, and the turning wheel comes to rest. What is most important is the removal of all suffering. Were the mantra unable to remove all suffering, it would not be of any great use. However, it can remove any suffering whatsoever – the three kinds of suffering, which are the suffering of suffering itself, the suffering of decay, and the suffering of the activity of the skandhas, and the eight kinds of suffering, which are the suffering of birth, the suffering of old age, the suffering of sickness, the suffering of death, the suffering of being apart from those you love, the suffering of being together with those you despise, the suffering of not obtaining what you seek, and the suffering of the flourishing of the five skandhas, which is the most difficult to remove, yet here it can also be removed. The mantra **can remove all suffering**. When "all suffering is removed, the turning wheel comes to rest."

If you can be liberated from the revolving wheel, then the wheel can stop. If you are not liberated from the turning wheel, then it cannot come to rest. You must end birth and death to leave the revolving wheel. "The turning wheel comes to rest," means the ending of birth and death.

How do you remove the three kinds of suffering and the eight kinds of suffering? How do you put an end to birth and death and get out of the revolving wheel? These five dwellings must be ended:

1) The suffering caused by love of views (also known as the affliction of the love of views);

2) The suffering caused by love of desire (also known as the affliction of the love of desire);

3) The suffering caused by love of form (also known as the affliction of the love of form);

4) The suffering caused by love of the formless (also known as the affliction of the love of the formless);

5) The suffering caused by love of ignorance (also known as the affliction of the love of ignorance).

There must be an end to the five dwellings, and the two deaths must disappear forever.

The five dwellings were described earlier. The word "dwelling" indicates solidity and durability, a place that does not move. Because of the solidity, a kind of craving arises in your mind for situations that you come face to face with. Before you have encountered the situation, the craving doesn't exist. As soon as you encounter it, the craving is generated. That is what is called dwelling in the affliction of the love of views. Dwelling in the love of desire refers to the heavens of the desire-realm. Dwelling in the love of form refers to the heavens of the form-realm, and dwelling in the love of the formless refers to the heavens of the formless realm. Although lifespans are long in the heavens of the formless realm, affliction and ignorance have not yet been cut off. These are called the five dwellings in affliction, because most people are very firmly attached to dwelling in them. If they were explained in detail, it would take a very long time to talk about them, so I am now just mentioning their names.

"The two deaths disappear forever." Some people who have not listened to sutras before hear "two deaths" and think, "Oh, do you have to die twice?" The reference is to the two kinds of dying, not to dying twice. As I explained earlier, there is the birth and death of the delimited segment and the birth and death of the fluctuations.

What is the birth and death of the delimited segment (in Chinese literally "share-section")? You have your share and I have my share; that is called "share." You have your body section and I have my body section; that is called "section." I am five feet eight inches tall, and there is a person here who is more than six feet tall. That is what is meant by you having your section and me having mine. This is what is called the birth and death of the delimited segment (i.e., of the share-section). From the day of birth to the day of death is a section, and from the bottom of your feet to the top of your head is also a section. Both are delimited segments. At the fourth stage of Arhatship, the birth and death of the delimited segment is cut off, but the birth and death of the fluctuations has not yet come to an end. Only the Bodhisattva is able to end the birth and death of the fluctuations.

"Genuine and not false": everyone progresses. The birth and death of the delimited segment and the birth and death of the fluctuations have come to an end. "The five dwellings are ended, and the two deaths disappear forever." That is genuine enlightenment. "All suffering is removed, and the turning wheel comes to rest:" that is the genuine Bodhisattva. "'Genuine and not false:" it's for certain that he isn't phony. "Everyone progresses" – immediately go forward in your cultivation. Do you want to be a Bodhisattva? Then go forward and cultivate. Go forward with diligence and vigor.

What has been spoken discloses the profound prajna. The section of the *Heart of Prajna Paramita Sutra* which has already been discussed was spoken exoterically, while the part that follows was spoken esoterically.

And briefly explains the dhyana of the Patriarchs of the East and West. The verses I wrote which have already been discussed briefly explain the meditational method of the Eastern and Western patriarchs. What method of meditation is it? The first verse on the text of the sutra said:

> *Reversing the light to shine within,*
>   *Avalokiteshvara*
> *Enlightens all the sentient beings;*
>   *thus he is a Bodhisattva.*

You should turn the light around to illuminate within. Everyone has the virtuous characteristic of the wisdom of the Thus Come One. But it is simply because of false thinking and attachment that ordinary people are unable to be certified as having attained it. If you wish to attain "the virtuous characteristic of the wisdom of the Thus Come One," you must not be attached. If you are capable of non-attachment, turn the light within. Study these verses so that you are reasonably familiar with them, and then sit and look into dhyana – meditate. The doctrine of the patriarchs of the East and of the West is simply that.

India is said to be the West, and China the East. But the East and West of the present are neither India nor China. East remains east and West west, of course; the directions have not moved or changed, but the situation has. East refers to the people of the East and West refers to the people of the West. The West will now give birth to a patriarch, and the Eastern patriarchs are quite numerous. There are so many of them that they are like water which flows to the West. Whoever wants to be a patriarch shouldn't sleep all the time; then it can be done. When one is awakened, East is not East and West is not West. North and South have also disappeared. Why? Now we have developed relations with the moon. So from this side, we don't know which side we are going to. There is no north, south, east, or west. Now we have all become the original one, the center. Yet the center has no center. This is to change into the great with nothing beyond and into the small with nothing within. It is what I spoke about earlier:

> There is no great or small,
> No inside or out;
> I cultivate, come to my end,
> And make the arrangements all by myself.

That's where you should get to. You should be able to do it and to see how wonderful it is. That is to truly have no troubles at all. Ultimately, what is it like when there is no great or small, no inside or out? If you already understand, you understand without my needing to say. If you don't understand and I tell you, you still won't understand.

Sutra:

That is why the mantra of prajna paramita was spoken. Recite it like this:

> *Gate gate paragate parasamgate bodhi svaha!*

Commentary:

Mantras are neither translated nor translatable. Since they fall under one of the five categories of terms which are not translated[43], it is unnecessary to talk about them. Their meanings are inconceivable.

Now I will talk about the mantra.

Verse:

> As part of the esoteric,
>   the mantra can't be thought about;
> It is followed by everyone together,
>   like the edict of a monarch
> And like a secret password among the troops.
> If one's reply to the question is not fitting,
>   one is quickly put in line.
> The wonderful truth of the Great Vehicle
>   is apart from distinctions,
> Yet ordinary people see false conditioned cause
>   as true.
> Guided by the finger, gaze at the moon;
>   the finger is not the moon;
> Borrowing the mantra, light the mind.
>   The mantra is the mind.

Commentary:

As part of the esoteric, the mantra can't be thought about. The mantra belongs to the esoteric teaching, which is inconceivable.

---

[43] Tang Dynasty Master of the Tripitaka Hsüan-tsang, whose translation of the *Heart Sutra* into Chinese is the basis of the present text, established five categories of words which should be left untranslated: the esoteric; words having multiple meanings; words for things not existing in China; words not translated in accord with already established precedent; and words left untranslated in order to give rise to whole-someness.

You cannot use any kind of thought to think about what it is. "The path of words is cut off, and the place of the mind and the nature is already destroyed"; there isn't a way to think about it even if you try.

It is followed by everyone together, like the edict of a monarch. This analogy is one of the four explained above. When a monarch sends down an edict, it is respectfully received by all the officials.

And like a secret password among the troops. It's as I said earlier: if the password for the day is "victory," and when challenged you say, "lucky," then the fighting begins, and they shoot you. Because there are so many people in the army, they use such secret passwords, one each day. In that way they don't mistake outsiders for their own people. Mantras have the same meaning.

If one's reply to the question is not fitting, one is quickly put in line. If you don't answer the password correctly, then they fulfill the responsibility of carrying out their orders.

The wonderful truth of the Great Vehicle is apart from distinctions. The Great Vehicle belongs to the Great Vehicle Dharma. Its wonderfully inconceivable principle contains no distinctions at all. It destroys all dharmas and is apart from all characteristics. Whatever is said disappears: that is prajna dharma. Whatever you say no longer exists after you say it.

Yet ordinary people see the false conditioned cause as true. Ordinary people suppose that their kinds of knowledge and views, that their viewpoints, which are generated by false thinking and self-seeking[44], are real. That is to mistake a thief for your own son. It is to be attached to everything which has a perceptible characteristic; it is to be attached to shadows.

Guided by the finger, gaze at the moon; the finger is not the moon. The sutra points out a road for you on which to cultivate the

---

[44.] *pan yuan* 攀緣, "climbing on conditions," i.e., scheming for one's own benefit.

Way. It is like pointing out the moon with a finger. For instance, someone points at the moon with his finger and says, "There's the moon." Supposing that the finger is the moon, you people look at the finger and not at the moon. But "The finger is not the moon"; you shouldn't think that it is. Although the sutra teaches you to cultivate the Way, you should not think that the sutra is the Way. Before you can have an attainment, it is necessary to cultivate the Way. You're wrong if you don't cultivate and if you suppose that the sutra is the Way.

Borrowing the mantra, light the mind. The mantra is the mind. Because the mantra is inconceivable, you can light up your mind by borrowing its power. You need only depart from the mind which makes distinctions, the self-seeking mind, the false-thinking mind, and recite the mantra and hold to it. To hold to the mantra is not to understand it, yet in that not understanding there can be true understanding. Therefore, borrowing the mantra enables you to light up your mind and see your nature. And "the mantra is the mind": if you light up your mind and see your nature, then you will also understand the mantra's meaning.

Index

A

activity-obstacle
  see three obstacles
affliction 95—105
  eight large subsidiary afflictions 99—
    103
  one produces infinity 110
  six basic 103—104
  ten small afflictions 96—98
  their number 95
  two middle-sized subsidiary afflictions
    98—99
  why is there...? 95
  see also Four Truths
affliction-obstacle
  see three obstacles
Agama period 14
  see five periods of the Buddha's
    teaching
Akshobhya Buddha 45
Amitabha Sutra 3
analogy
  of precious pearl 4
  of the cylindrical net-curtain 3
anger 103
  see also affliction, six basic
annihilation 31, 74
annoyance 96
  see also affliction, ten small
Arhatship 45
  ending birth and death 32
  first stage 44
  fourth stage 32, 107, 151

arrogance 98, 104
  see also affliction, six basic
  see also affliction, ten small
asuras 139
attachment
  letting go 134
  to attainment 126
  to body is false 37—38
  to defilement and purity 72—74
  to the five dwellings 151
Avalokiteshvara Bodhisattva 128
Avalokiteshvara, Bodhisattva 23, 29—30
Avatamsaka period 14
  see five periods of the Buddha's
    teaching
Avatamsaka Sutra 5, 92

B

birth and death
  afraid of 109
  and Bodhisattvas 130
  are one 83
  does not exist 130
  ending 32, 45, 77, 106—108, 131
  of the delimited segment 151
  of the fluctuations 152
  two kinds 32
Bodhisattva 24, 25, 127—131
  and supreme enlightenment 141
  birth and death 32, 45, 130
  genuine 129, 152
  ten grounds 128
Book of Changes

see I Ching
Brahma Net Sutra 3, 4, 5
Buddhadharma
    is tasty! 76
Buddhahood 57
    Great Expanse 5
    realizing, via precepts 4
    uniting with 37
butter division
    see prajna period

C

Cao Creek 49
cognition 65
Conditioned-Enlightened 139, 141
Condition-Enlightened Vehicle 84
cultivation 127, 142

D

Da Xiu, the Monk 134
Dao-sheng, Dharma Master 135
defilement and purity 72–74
dependent retribution 9, 10
Dharma Lotus Flower Sutra 81, 82
dharmas
    are empty of characteristics 8
dhyana 108
dhyana samadhi 121
    see also paramitas, phenomenal and
        noumenal
disbelief 99
    see also affliction, eight large
distraction 103
    see also affliction, eight large
doubt 104
    see also affliction, six basic
dreaming 54–55, 139
drowsiness 101

see also affliction, eight large

E

Earth Store Bodhisattva 128
earthquake, in San Francisco 22
eight kinds of suffering 41–42
eight mind-dharmas 70
eight winds 27–28
eighteen fields, the 80
eightfold upright path 116
    see also Way, thirty-seven categoris
emptiness
    analogy of ice and water 58
    and existence 79
    and the four great elements 37
    cultivating 40–41
    is form 51–54, 57–59, 69, 79
    of form and feeling 37–39
    of the five skandhas 39, 43
    see five kinds of emptiness
enlightenment
    and false-thinking 90
    small, middle and great 76–77
enmity 96
    see also affliction, ten small
eternalism 74
existence
    and emptiness 79

F

false-thinking 90
feelings 64–65
five categories of recondite meaning 6–
    12
five dwellings 45, 150–151
five faculties 118
    see also Way, thirty-seven categoris
five kinds of emptiness 31–33

five perceptual faculties 68
five periods of the Buddha's teaching 14—
   15
five powers 118
   see also Way, thirty-seven categoris
five skandhas 60, 66—67, 70
   are empty 39, 70
flattery, obsequious 97
   see also affliction, ten small
form 63—64
   analogy of ice and water 58
   is emptiness 51—54, 57—59, 69, 79
   see form-skandha
formation 65
form-dharmas 30, 31, 54, 70
   complimentary and invisible 68
form-skandha 62
   three categories 59—61
four attainments of Nirvana 106
four bases of psychic power 117
   see also Way, thirty-seven categoris
four dwellings in mindfulness 117
   see also Way, thirty-seven categoris
four great elements 37
four teachings 128
Four Truths 44
   accumulating 105
   emptying 91—113
   extinction 106—108
   suffering 94—95
   the three turnings 93—94
   the Way 108—113
   see also affliction
four types of upright deligence
   see also Way, thirty-seven categoris
four types of upright diligence 117
Fo-yin, Great Master
   and Su Dong Po 27

G

gambling 67
ghost-kings 145
ghosts 10, 56
giving 120
   see also paramitas, phenomenal and
      noumenal
god 56
god-kings 145
Great Brahma Heaven 3
Great Prajna Sutra 8
greed 103
   see also affliction, six basic

H

Hearers 141
   see shravakas
Heart of Prajna Paramita Sutra 5, 7
   see Heart Sutra
Heart Sutra 8, 16, 79, 139
   a great bright mantra 149
   basic purpose 9
   can remove the three obstacles 12
Hinayana 15, 30
Hsu Yun, Venerable Master 123
Hsüan Tsang, Dharma Master 20—21
Hui Neng, Great Master 58
humility, lack of 99
   see also affliction, two middle-sized

I

I Ching 44, 111
ignorance 84
   see twelve conditioned causes
impediments 134

J

jealousy 98
   see also affliction, ten small
Jewelled Wood Mountain 50
Judgment Day
   see Last Day

K

knowledge, improper 102
   see also affliction, eight large
kumbhanda 145
Kwangtung Province 49

L

language, secret 146
   see mantra
Last Day 21—22
laxity 100
   see also affliction, eight large
Lion's Roar of the Thus Come One Sutra
   5
Lotus Flower Sutra 25
Lotus-Nirvana period 15
   see five periods of the Buddha's
      teaching
lying 97
   see also affliction, ten small

M

Ma-ba Township 49
Mahaparinirvana Sutra 12, 15
Mahayana 15
Maitreya Bodhisattva 70
malevolence 98
   see also affliction, ten small
Manjushri Asks about Prajna Sutra 5
Manjushri Bodhisattva 128

mantra 144—156
   are not translated 154
   four meanings 145—147
   Heart Sutra 149
   is esoteric 154
   is hard to fathom 148
   removes suffering 150
mind-dharmas 30, 31
mindfulness, loss of 102
   see also affliction, eight large
mind-seals 147
   see mantras
mountain essences 10

N

Nagarjuna Bodhisattva
   describes extinction 72
   describes production 71
Nan-hua Monastery 49
net-curtain
   see analogy of the cylindrical net-cur-
      tain
Nirvana 139—140
   four attainments 106
Nirvana Sutra 3
non-attainment 9

O

old spirits 10
outflows 4
   extinction of 137

P

paramitas
   six phenomenal and noumenal 120—
      122
past lives
   remembering 55

patience under insult 121
  see also paramitas, phenomenal and
    noumenal
people
  fame and fortune 139
  two types of 10
permanence 74
pisaca 145
prajna 121
  profound and superficial 30
  three types of 7
  see also paramitas, phenomenal and
    noumenal
prajna paramita 8, 29–33
Prajna period 12, 15
  see five periods of the Buddha's
    teaching
Prasenajit, King 132
Pratyekabuddhas 139
precepts 3, 4, 20, 48
  maintaining 114, 120
    see also paramitas, phenomenal
      and noumenal
  of a Bodhisattva 4
  prohibitive 107
  see analogy of precious pearl
precious pearl
  see analogy of precious pearl
pride 104
  see also affliction, six basic
primary retribution 9, 10
production and extinction 71–74
purity
  see defilement and purity

R

reciting sutras 16–17
repression 97
  see also affliction, ten small

restless inattention 101
  see also affliction, eight large
retribution
  see primary, dependent retribution
  see Shakyamuni Buddha, retribution
retribution-obstacle
  see three obstacles

S

saindhava 147
Samantabhadra Bodhisattva 128
San Francisco, earthquake 22
secret language 146
  see mantra
sentient beings 127
seven categories of titles 3–5
seven shares in enlightenment 114
  see also Way, thirty-seven categoris
sexual behavior 85
shadow 56, 68
Shakyamuni Buddha
  and the Avatamsaka Sutra 92
  horse-feed retribution 42
  metal-spear retribution 41
shame, lack of 99
  see also affliction, two middle-sized
Shariputra 47–49
shastras
  see Tripitaka
Shi, Emperor
  and elixir of immortality 44
shravakas 92, 139
Shurangama Mantra 22, 127
Shurangama Sutra 88, 92
six paths of rebirth 43
six psychic powers 26, 137
skandha
  see five skandhas
  see form-skandha

Song, country 88
spleen 82
stinginess 98
    see also affliction, ten small
stupidity 104
    and the prajna-boat 12
    see also affliction, six basic
    see Song, country
Su Dong Po, poet
    and Fo-yin, Great Master 26—27
suffering 40—46
    eight kinds of 41—42
    the more, the better 77
    three kinds of 41
    see Four Truths
sutras
    are without any characteristics 8
    lecturing 135
    only point to the Way 156
    reciting 16—17
    titles, meaning of 16—19
    see Tripitaka

T

thirty-seven categories of the Way 113—
    118
three forces 36
three kinds of feeling 41
three kinds of form 68
    see form-skandha
three kinds of suffering 41, 94
three lights 35
three minds, the 81
three obstacles 9—12, 126
    activity-obstacle 11
    affliction-obstacle 11—12
    retribution-obstacle 9—11
three storehouses
    see Tripitaka 20

three turnings of the dharma wheel 93—94
time
    neither increases nor decreases 76
    past, present and future 81
    stealing 135
torpor 100
    see also affliction, eight large
translator, the
    see Hsuan Tsang, Dharma Master
Tripitaka 20
true heart 7
true mind 7
twelve conditioned causes 84—90
twelve dwellings, the 80
two kinds of wisdom 14

U

upset 96
    see also affliction, ten small

V

Vaipulya period 15
    see five periods of the Buddha's
        teaching
vehicle
    small, middle and great 84
views, deviant 104
    see also affliction, six basic
vigor 121, 142
    see also paramitas, phenomenal and
        noumenal
vinaya
    see Tripitaka

W

Way, the 108—113
    thirty-seven categories 113—118
Western Paradise 45

Y

yellow-faced child 82

Buddhist Text Translation Society Publication

Buddhist Text Translation Society
International Translation Institute

http://www.bttsonline.org

1777 Murchison Drive,
Burlingame, California 94010-4504 USA
Phone: 650-692-5912 Fax: 650-692-5056

When Buddhism first came to China from India, one of the most important tasks required for its establishment was the translation of the Buddhist scriptures from Sanskrit into Chinese. This work involved a great many people, such as the renowned monk National Master Kumarajiva (fifth century), who led an assembly of over 800 people to work on the translation of the Tripitaka (Buddhist canon) for over a decade. Because of the work of individuals such as these, nearly the entire Buddhist Tripitaka of over a thousand texts exists to the present day in Chinese.

Now the banner of the Buddha's Teachings is being firmly planted in Western soil, and the same translation work is being done from Chinese into English. Since 1970, the Buddhist Text Translation Society (BTTS) has been making a paramount contribution toward this goal. Aware that the Buddhist Tripitaka is a work of such magnitude that its translation could never be entrusted to a single person, the BTTS, emulating the translation assemblies of ancient times, does not publish a work until it has passed through four committees for primary translation, revision, editing, and certification. The leaders of these committees are Bhikshus (monks) and Bhikshunis (nuns) who have devoted their lives to the study and practice of the Buddha's teachings. For this reason, all of the works of the BTTS put an emphasis on what the principles of the Buddha's teachings mean in terms of actual practice and not simply hypothetical conjecture.

The translations of canonical works by the Buddhist Text Translation Society are accompanied by extensive commentaries by the Venerable Tripitaka Master Hsuan Hua.

BTTS Publications

Buddhist Sutras. Amitabha Sutra, Dharma Flower (Lotus) Sutra, Flower Adornment (Avatamsaka) Sutra, Heart Sutra & Verses without a Stand, Shurangama Sutra, Sixth Patriarch Sutra, Sutra in Forty-two Sections, Sutra of the Past Vows of Earth Store Bodhisattva, Vajra Prajna Paramita (Diamond) Sutra.

Commentarial Literature. Buddha Root Farm, City of 10 000 Buddhas Recitation Handbook, Filiality: The Human Source, Herein Lies the Treasure-trove, Listen to Yourself Think Everything Over, Shastra on the Door to Understanding the Hundred Dharmas, Song of Enlightenment, The Ten Dharma Realms Are Not Beyond a Single Thought, Venerable Master Hua's Talks on Dharma, Venerable Master Hua's Talks on Dharma during the 1993 Trip to Taiwan, Water Mirror Reflecting Heaven.

Biographical. In Memory of the Venerable Master Hsuan Hua, Pictorial Biography of the Venerable Master Hsü Yün, Records of High Sanghans, Records of the Life of the Venerable Master Hsüan Hua, Three Steps One Bow, World Peace Gathering, News from True Cultivators, Open Your Eyes Take a Look at the World, With One Heart Bowing to the City of 10 000 Buddhas.

Children's Books. Cherishing Life, Human Roots: Buddhist Stories for Young Readers, Spider Web, Giant Turtle, Patriarch Bodhidharma.

Musics, Novels and Brochures. Songs for Awakening, Awakening, The Three Cart Patriarch, City of 10 000 Buddhas Color Brochure, Celebrisi's Journey, Lots of Time Left.

The Buddhist Monthly–Vajra Bodhi Sea is a monthly journal of orthodox Buddhism which has been published by the Dharma Realm Buddhist Association, formerly known as the Sino-American Buddhist Association, since 1970. Each issue contains the most recent translations of the Buddhist canon by the Buddhist Text Translation Society. Also included in each issue are a biography of a great Patriarch of Buddhism from the ancient past, sketches of the lives of contemporary monastics and lay-followers around the world, articles on practice, and other material. The journal is bilingual, Chinese and English

Please visit our web-site at **www.bttsonline.org** for the latest publications and for ordering information.

The Dharma Realm Buddhist Association

Mission

The Dharma Realm Buddhist Association (formerly the Sino-American Buddhist Association) was founded by the Venerable Master Hsuan Hua in the United States of America in 1959. Taking the Dharma Realm as its scope, the Association aims to disseminate the genuine teachings of the Buddha throughout the world. The Association is dedicated to translating the Buddhist canon, propagating the Orthodox Dharma, promoting ethical education, and bringing benefit and happiness to all beings. Its hope is that individuals, families, the society, the nation, and the entire world will, under the transforming influence of the Buddhadharma, gradually reach the state of ultimate truth and goodness.

The Founder

The Venerable Master, whose names were An Tse and To Lun, received the Dharma name Hsuan Hua and the transmission of Dharma from Venerable Master Hsu Yun in the lineage of the Wei Yang Sect. He was born in Manchuria, China, at the beginning of the century. At nineteen, he entered the monastic order and dwelt in a hut by his mother's grave to practice filial piety. He meditated, studied the teachings, ate only one meal a day, and slept sitting up. In 1948 he went to Hong Kong, where he established the Buddhist Lecture Hall and other Way-places. In 1962 he brought the Proper Dharma to the West, lecturing on several dozen Mahayana Sutras in the United States. Over the years, the Master established more than twenty monasteries of Proper Dharma under the auspices of the Dharma Realm Buddhist Association and the City of Ten Thousand Buddhas. He also founded centers for the translation of the Buddhist canon and for education to spread the influence of the Dharma in the East and West. The Master manifested the stillness in the United States in 1995. Through his lifelong, selfless dedication to teaching living beings with wisdom and compassion, he influenced countless people to change their faults and to walk upon the pure, bright path to enlightenment.

Dharma Propagation, Buddhist Text Translation, and Education

The Venerable Master Hua's three great vows after leaving the home-life were (1) to propagate the Dharma, (2) to translate the Buddhist Canon, and (3) to promote education. In order to make these vows a reality, the Venerable Master based himself on the Three Principles and the Six Guidelines. Courageously facing every hardship, he founded monasteries, schools, and centers in the West, drawing in living beings and teaching them on a vast scale. Over the years, he founded the following institutions:

The City of Ten Thousand Buddhas and Its Branches

In propagating the Proper Dharma, the Venerable Master not only trained people but also founded Way-places where the Dharma wheel could turn and living beings could be saved. He wanted to provide cultivators with pure places to practice in accord with the Buddha's regulations. Over the years, he founded many Way-places of Proper Dharma. In the United States and Canada, these include the City of Ten Thousand Buddhas; Gold Mountain Monastery; Gold Sage Monastery; Gold Wheel Monastery; Gold Summit Monastery; Gold Buddha Monastery; Avatamsaka Monastery; Long Beach Monastery; the City of the Dharma Realm; Berkeley Buddhist Monastery; Avatamsaka Hermitage; and Blessings, Prosperity, and Longevity Monastery. In Taiwan, there are the Dharma Realm Buddhist Books Distribution Association, Dharma Realm Monastery, and Amitabha Monastery. In Malaysia, there are the Prajna Guanyin Sagely Monastery (formerly Tze Yun Tung Temple), Deng Bi An Monastery, and Lotus Vihara. In Hong Kong, there are the Buddhist Lecture Hall and Cixing Monastery.

Purchased in 1974, the City of Ten Thousand Buddhas is the hub of the Dharma Realm Buddhist Association. The City is located in Talmage, Mendocino County, California, 110 miles north of San Francisco. Eighty of the 488 acres of land are in active use. The remaining acreage consists of meadows, orchards, and woods. With over seventy large buildings containing over 2,000 rooms, blessed with serenity and fresh, clean air, it is the first large Buddhist monastic community in the United States. It is also an international center for the Proper Dharma.

Although the Venerable Master Hua was the Ninth Patriarch in the Wei Yang Sect of the Chan School, the monasteries he founded emphasize all of the five main practices of Mahayana Buddhism (Chan meditation, Pure Land, esoteric, Vinaya (moral discipline), and doctrinal studies). This accords with the Buddha's words: "The Dharma is level and equal, with no high or low." At the City of Ten Thousand Buddhas, the rules of purity are rigorously observed. Residents of the City strive to regulate their own conduct and to cultivate with vigor. Taking refuge in the Proper Dharma, they lead pure and selfless lives, and attain peace in body and mind. The Sutras are expounded and the Dharma wheel is turned daily. Residents dedicate themselves wholeheartedly to making Buddhism flourish. Monks and nuns in all the monasteries take one meal a day, always wear their precept sash, and follow the Three Principles:

Freezing, we do not scheme.
Starving, we do not beg.
Dying of poverty, we ask for nothing.
According with conditions, we do not change.
Not changing, we accord with conditions.
We adhere firmly to our three great principles.
We renounce our lives to do the Buddha's work.
We take the responsibility to mold our own destinies.
We rectify our lives to fulfill the Sanghan's role.
Encountering specific matters,
  we understand the principles.
Understanding the principles,
  we apply them in specific matters.
We carry on the single pulse of
  the Patriarchs' mind-transmission.

The monasteries also follow the Six Guidelines: not contending, not being greedy, not seeking, not being selfish, not pursuing personal advantage, and not lying.

International Translation Institute

The Venerable Master vowed to translate the Buddhist Canon (Tripitaka) into Western languages so that it would be widely accessible throughout the world. In 1973, he founded the International Translation Institute on Washington Street in San Francisco for the purpose of translating Buddhist scriptures into English and other languages. In 1977, the Institute was merged into Dharma Realm Buddhist University as the Institute for the Translation of Buddhist Texts. In 1991, the Venerable Master purchased a large building in Burlingame (south of San Francisco) and established the International Translation Institute there for the purpose of translating and publishing Buddhist texts. To date, in addition to publishing over one hundred volumes of Buddhist texts in Chinese, the Association has published more than one hundred volumes of English, French, Spanish, Vietnamese, and Japanese translations of Buddhist texts, as well as bilingual (Chinese and English) editions. Audio and video tapes also continue to be produced. The monthly journal Vajra Bodhi Sea, which has been in circulation for nearly thirty years, has been published in bilingual (Chinese and English) format in recent years.

In the past, the difficult and vast mission of translating the Buddhist canon in China was sponsored and supported by the emperors and kings themselves. In our time, the Venerable Master encouraged his disciples to cooperatively shoulder this heavy responsibility, producing books and audio tapes and using the medium of language to turn the wheel of Proper Dharma and do the great work of the Buddha. All those who aspire to devote themselves to this work of sages should uphold the Eight Guidelines of the International Translation Institute:

1. One must free oneself from the motives of personal fame and profit.
2. One must cultivate a respectful and sincere attitude free from arrogance and conceit.
3. One must refrain from aggrandizing one's work and denigrating that of others.
4. One must not establish oneself as the standard of correctness and suppress the work of others with one's fault-finding.
5. One must take the Buddha-mind as one's own mind.
6. One must use the wisdom of Dharma-Selecting Vision to determine true principles.
7. One must request Virtuous Elders of the ten directions to certify one's translations.
8. One must endeavor to propagate the teachings by printing Sutras, Shastra texts, and Vinaya texts when the translations are certified as being correct.

These are the Venerable Master's vows, and participants in the work of translation should strive to realize them.

Instilling Goodness Elementary School, Developing Virtue Secondary School, Dharma Realm Buddhist University

"Education is the best national defense." The Venerable Master Hua saw clearly that in order to save the world, it is essential to promote good education. If we want to save the world, we have to bring about a complete change in people's minds and guide them to cast out unwholesomeness and to pursue goodness. To this end the Master founded Instilling Goodness Elementary School in 1974, and Developing Virtue Secondary School and Dharma Realm Buddhist University in 1976.

In an education embodying the spirit of Buddhism, the elementary school teaches students to be filial to parents, the secondary school teaches students to be good citizens, and the university teaches such virtues as humaneness and righteousness. Instilling Goodness Elementary School and Developing Virtue Secondary School combine the best of contemporary and traditional methods and of Western and Eastern cultures. They emphasize moral virtue and spiritual development, and aim to guide students to become good and capable citizens who will benefit humankind. The schools offer a bilingual (Chinese/English) program where boys and girls study separately. In addition to standard academic courses, the curriculum includes ethics, meditation, Buddhist studies, and so on, giving students a foundation in virtue and guiding them to understand themselves and explore the truths of the universe. Branches of the schools (Sunday schools) have been established at branch monasteries with the aim of propagating filial piety and ethical education.

Dharma Realm Buddhist University, whose curriculum focuses on the Proper Dharma, does not merely transmit academic knowledge. It emphasizes a foundation in virtue, which expands into the study of how to help all living beings discover their inherent nature. Thus, Dharma Realm Buddhist University advocates a spirit of shared inquiry and free exchange of ideas, encouraging students to study various canonical texts and use different experiences and learning styles to tap their inherent wisdom and fathom the meanings of those texts. Students are encouraged to practice the principles they have understood and apply the Buddhadharma in their lives, thereby nurturing their wisdom and virtue. The University aims to produce outstanding individuals of high moral character who will be able to bring benefit to all sentient beings.

Sangha and Laity Training Programs

In the Dharma-ending Age, in both Eastern and Western societies there are very few monasteries that actually practice the Buddha's regulations and strictly uphold the precepts. Teachers with genuine wisdom and understanding, capable of guiding those who aspire to pursue careers in Buddhism, are very rare. The Venerable Master founded the Sangha and Laity Training Programs in 1982 with the goals of raising the caliber of the Sangha, perpetuating the Proper Dharma, providing professional training for Buddhists around the world on both practical and theoretical levels, and transmitting the wisdom of the Buddha.

The Sangha Training Program gives monastics a solid foundation in Buddhist studies and practice, training them in the practical affairs of Buddhism and Sangha management. After graduation, students will be able to assume various responsibilities related to Buddhism in monasteries, institutions, and other settings. The program emphasizes a thorough knowledge of Buddhism, understanding of the scriptures, earnest cultivation, strict observance of precepts, and the development of a virtuous character, so that students will be able to propagate the Proper Dharma and perpetuate the Buddha's wisdom. The Laity Training Program offers courses to help laypeople develop correct views, study and practice the teachings, and understand monastic regulations and ceremonies, so that they will be able to contribute their abilities in Buddhist organizations.

Let Us Go Forward Together

In this Dharma-ending Age when the world is becoming increasingly dangerous and evil, the Dharma Realm Buddhist Association, in consonance with its guiding principles, opens the doors of its monasteries and centers to those of all religions and nationalities. Anyone who is devoted to humaneness, righteousness, virtue, and the pursuit of truth, and who wishes to understand him or herself and help humankind, is welcome to come study and practice with us. May we together bring benefit and happiness to all living beings.

Dharma Realm Buddhist Association Branches

The City of Ten Thousand Buddhas
P.O. Box 217, Talmage, CA 95481-0217 USA
Tel: (707) 462-0939   Fax: (707) 462-0949
Home Page: http://www.drba.org

Institute for World Religions (Berkeley Buddhist Monastery)
2304 McKinley Avenue, Berkeley, CA 94703 USA
Tel: (510) 848-3440

Dharma Realm Buddhist Books Distribution Society
11th Floor, 85 Chung-hsiao E. Road, Sec. 6, Taipei, Taiwan R.O.C.
Tel: (02) 2786-3022 Fax: (02) 2786-2674

The City of the Dharma Realm
1029 West Capitol Avenue, West Sacramento, CA 95691 USA
Tel: (916) 374-8268

Gold Mountain Monastery
800 Sacramento Street, San Francisco, CA 94108 USA
Tel: (415) 421-6117 Fax: (415) 788-6001

Gold Wheel Monastery
235 North Avenue 58, Los Angeles, CA 90042 USA
Tel: (323) 258-6668

Gold Buddha Monastery
248 East 11th Avenue, Vancouver, B.C. V5T 2C3 Canada
Tel: (604) 709-0248 Fax: (604) 684-3754

Gold Summit Monastery
233 1st Avenue, West Seattle, WA 98119 USA
Tel: (206) 284-6690 Fax: (206) 284-6918

Gold Sage Monastery
11455 Clayton Road, San Jose, CA 95127 USA
Tel: (408) 923-7243 Fax: (408) 923-1064

The International Translation Institute
1777 Murchison Drive, Burlingame, CA 94010-4504 USA
Tel: (650) 692-5912 Fax: (650) 692-5056

Long Beach Monastery
3361 East Ocean Boulevard, Long Beach, CA 90803 USA
Tel: (562) 438-8902

Blessings, Prosperity, & Longevity Monastery
4140 Long Beach Boulevard, Long Beach, CA 90807 USA
Tel: (562) 595-4966

Avatamsaka Hermitage
11721 Beall Mountain Road, Potomac, MD 20854-1128 USA
Tel: (301) 299-3693

Avatamsaka Monastery
1009 4th Avenue, S.W. Calgary, AB T2P OK8 Canada
Tel: (403) 234-0644 Email: ava@nucleus.com

Kun Yam Thong Temple
161, Jalan Ampang, 50450 Kuala Lumpur, Malaysia
Tel: (03) 2164-8055 Fax: (03) 2163-7118

Prajna Guanyin Sagely Monastery (formerly Tze Yun Tung)
Batu 5½, Jalan Sungai Besi,
Salak Selatan, 57100 Kuala Lumpur, Malaysia
Tel: (03) 7982-6560 Fax: (03) 7980-1272

Lotus Vihara
136, Jalan Sekolah, 45600 Batang Berjuntai,
Selangor Darul Ehsan, Malaysia
Tel: (03) 3271-9439

Buddhist Lecture Hall
31 Wong Nei Chong Road, Top Floor, Happy Valley, Hong Kong, China
Tel: (02) 2572-7644

Dharma Realm Sagely Monastery
20, Tong-hsi Shan-chuang, Hsing-lung Village, Liu-kuei
Kaohsiung County, Taiwan, R.O.C.
Tel: (07) 689-3717 Fax: (07) 689-3870

Amitabha Monastery
7, Su-chien-hui, Chih-nan Village, Shou-feng,
Hualien County, Taiwan, R.O.C.
Tel: (07) 865-1956 Fax: (07) 865-3426

Verse of Transference

May the merit and virtue accrued from this work,
Adorn the Buddhas' Pure Lands,
Repaying four kinds of kindness above,
And aiding those suffering in the paths below.

May those who see and hear of this,
All bring forth the resolve for Bodhi,
And when this retribution body is over,
Be born together in the Land of Ultimate Bliss.

Dharma Protector Wei Tuo Bodhisattva

$127